CYGNUS

PEGASUS

CEPHES

OLARIS

CASSIOPEIA

TAURUS

ORION

D0578079

the **Night School**

the Night School

LESSONS IN MOONLIGHT, MAGIC, AND THE MYSTERIES OF BEING HUMAN

MAIA TOLL

illustrated by LUCILLE CLERC

RUNNING PRESS

PHILADELPHIA

Running Press
Hachette Book Group
1290 Avenue of the Americas, New York, NY 10104
www.runningpress.com
@Running_Press

Printed in Singapore

First Edition: August 2022

The origin story on page 32 is courtesy *The Oneida Creation Story*,
published by Bison Books/University of Nebraska Press.

Published by Running Press, an imprint of Perseus Books, LLC, a subsidiary
of Hachette Book Group, Inc. The Running Press name and logo is a trademark
of the Hachette Book Group.

The Hachette Speakers Bureau provides a wide range of authors
for speaking events. To find out more, go to www.hachettespeakersbureau.com
or call (866) 376-6591.

The publisher is not responsible for websites (or their content)
that are not owned by the publisher.

Print book cover and interior design by Susan Van Horn

LCCN: 2021028799

ISBNs: 978-0-7624-7429-5 (hardcover), 978-0-7624-7428-8 (ebook),
978-1-6686-0589-9 (audio)

COS

10 9 8 7 6 5 4 3 2 1

There are no answers,
only questions enough
to fill the Night sky.

—Bea Marlowe,
The Night Mistress

contents

magic is everywhere.

To see it and the

effects it has on your life,

change the way you

perceive the world.

To harness it,

change the way you interact

with the energies around you.

To know it,

change the way you think.

To live it,

remember the lessons of the

Night as you go about your day.

ORIENTATION

Welcome to the Night School

IMAGINE FOR A MOMENT THAT YOU'RE SNUGGLED INTO A window seat, enjoying the night's lights as your plane descends into your favorite city. Maybe it's Paris and you can pick out the golden blaze of the 336 sodium floodlights that adorn the Eiffel Tower. Nearby you see a string of smaller lights that ignite your imagination with images of people chatting and laughing in the Left Bank's sidewalk cafes.

This is the magic of the modern world, Firefly. It's a beautiful magic, full of convenience and ease, but it's so well-lit there's little room for mystery. The night, with the advent of the electric light, has become as illuminated as the day.

But in the time before streetlights and headlights the Night was something else: a place of speculation, myth, and metaphor that could be accessed simply by stepping outside and blinking on your Night vision. This is literal: your eyes actually have Night mode! But if you're like many North Americans and Europeans, you probably rarely use it. With the prevalence of electric lights, most of us have forgotten how to switch on our Night sight and have simultaneously lost the soft wonder that comes with it.

But beyond the glow of electric lights, the evening hours become what they've always been: a breath of mystery, a time when reality tastes different on your tongue. As daylight fades, it's possible to step into the mystic and know the many shades of gray that make up both the universe and your own psyche.

Welcome to the Night School, Firefly.

You've been chosen, through your own rigorous self-examination, to matriculate into this esteemed program. If you're here, you're ready to see the universe for all its beautiful complexity.

The Night is not a place of absolutes. As you slide into these pages, dare to question your daytime truths and what you think you know or believe. Ask yourself to avoid the linear: think instead in circles and spirals and shooting stars. Every question you ponder will lead you closer not to *the* truth but to *your* truth.

At the Night School, you'll learn about the lure of ancient symbolism and how it speaks to your individual spirit, while simultaneously nodding toward a shared universal experience. You'll explore your internal cycles and those of the world around you. You'll follow threads of inquiry back through the ages, tracking thought forms through time and connecting the dots *for yourself*, so you can craft your own kind of magic.

Best of all, none of this needs to make sense by the light of day. The logic of light has nothing to do with the dream spaces of Night's darkness. The Night School curriculum is full of gentle magic and the lore of the mystics. Don't think too hard. Simply follow the strands of intuition and inner knowing. If you find yourself jumping up from reading a lesson to rediscover a photograph you haven't looked at in a decade or to read a poem you remember from college, you're on the right track. If you suddenly need to understand the imagery of snakes or how fire has been used in rituals around the globe, your studies are progressing stellarly.

By diving into the unknown you'll find not only yourself, but also the lost magic of the world and the place where serendipity lives.

Your Night School lessons are delivered in bite-sized bits perfect for pondering in the evening hours. Challenge yourself to study by candlelight so you can experience the liminal spaces where the light and dark commingle.

(Don't be a modern romantic about this, Firefly: a zillion tea lights all over the house are a good way to burn it down. Your great, great, great grandmother used a sturdy glass lantern for a reason.)

Many lessons contained in this book have homework: something to dream on or look up, a list to make, or a passage to read. At the end of each unit you'll find additional resources. These are longer journeys: you can't make it there and back in a Night. Sprinkle some extra credit into your studies as you see fit. They're the marshmallows in the cocoa, sometimes adding depth and richness to the flavor, but at other times turning something that had been tasty into sugary goo. Use your best judgment (always).

Let's discover the rhythms of your own inner knowing. Fuzzy slippers are encouraged, and mud masks are allowed. Read no more than one lesson each evening, giving yourself space to dream on the images, symbols, and concepts you'll encounter.

It's time to sip the Moon Juice!
Bea Marlowe, The Night Mistress

Your Only Prerequisite

This is the most important lesson, Firefly.

This is the lesson that stitches together all of the teachings to come. It's the foundation for everything that will follow in your Night School curriculum, so write it out, tape it to your bathroom mirror, and read it every morning and evening while you brush your teeth.

Ready?

> *Magic is everywhere.*
> *To see it and the effects it has on your life,*
> *change the way you perceive the world.*
> *To harness it,*
> *change the way you interact with the energies*
> *around you.*
> *To know it,*
> *change the way you think.*
> *To live it,*
> *remember the lessons of the Night as you go*
> *about your day.*

This mantra is your starting point. If you get stuck as you work through your lessons, return to this precept. Meditate on the words and allow them to open you back up to the mystic.

If you've hit a roadblock in your studies, it probably means that you've reverted to previous thought patterns. Old thought forms are like a pair of well-worn pajamas: they're so comfortable they're hard to get rid of, even when they're full of holes. Use the Night School mantra to, quite literally, change your mind. (Minds are amazingly malleable and truly don't mind being changed!)

Still, go easy on yourself. Most likely you grew up in a daylight culture and your brain is used to understanding the world based on strict daylight logic. But the Night is vast and mysterious; it requires nonlinear thought. The Night exists to balance the day, and so, to balance yourself, you must give space to the darkness. But never fear: as you break them in, your new thought forms will become soft, soothing, and easy to sleep in.

On that note, let's step into the Night!

Gather Your Supplies

It's back-to-school time!

I've compiled a list of the materials required to complete your Night School curriculum. You won't need everything right away: the list is divided by semester and I'll remind you halfway along what to gather for the second part of your coursework.

Don't panic if there are items listed you don't have on hand. You needn't do extensive shopping. Following the list version, I'll go over each item in detail, including substitutions and homemade options. Peruse the detailed descriptions before you run out and acquire something fancy! It's lovely to have beautiful tools, but ultimately, the tool is not what matters: an ugly hammer hits a nail just as well as a svelte one. (Unless it doesn't—a pretty frippery that can't drive a nail is useless, so be sure that your tools are up to the tasks they're being enlisted to perform!)

Supplies for all Night School Studies

* a journal
* candles
* a window, deck, porch, front stoop, sit spot, or meadow
* a pocket compass

Additional Supplies for Semester 1

  * Nothing beyond your general supplies listed above, a pinch
    of gumption, and a cup or two of salt

Additional Supplies for Semester 2

  * a rattle
  * a pendulum
  * an herb bundle
  * a tarot or oracle deck
  * a scrying mirror
  * ingredients for
    Bananas Foster
  * an ephemeris
  * a star map

A JOURNAL

Your most important tool is your journal . . . so make sure you actually
like the one you plan to use! There are many types of books you can write
in: a notebook with lines or a sketchbook without; something spiral-bound
or something stitched; a small journal that fits in your pocket or a big
notebook that sits across your knees. Your journal should make you want
to write or doodle or draw. Treat yourself to *your* journal, Firefly. Stepping
into the Night requires that you embrace symbolism. Your journal is a
symbol: it will remind you of *who you are, who you want to become*, and
what's important to you.

This special, carefully chosen journal will become your mystical recipe
book—written by the most reliable source: *you.*

CANDLES

In addition to your journal, you'll want a few candles to light your way. Be
sure these candles are contained, so you can focus on your lessons and
not worry about wrangling errant sparks. Candles should be beeswax or
soy, either unscented or scented with essential oils (not fragrance oils).
Why? Because you're working on your connection to the natural world,

Firefly, so you need to surround yourself with natural stuff. Plus, one of your main tasks at the Night School is to question what's served up to you by the light of day. Start this process by looking up "synthetic fragrance and neurology." Read a few articles. Yes, this is required homework: it's important to understand what intriguing scents like "Forest Suede" and "Pinnacle Peach" are doing to your neurons!

Extra Credit

Choose candles of differing colors and scents so you can see how using these variants affects your studies. When you change the candle's color, does it impact your mood? Your level of focus? Does color choice affect how relaxed you are or how lively your imagination feels? This is an experiment. Scientific method demands you go in with an open mind and simply record the results. Close *Mrs. Heggleworth's Guide to Candle Magic.* Simply see what happens for you . . . then write it down.

Experiments are verified by repetition,
so don't assume something is true
until you have gotten the same result
multiple times.

A WINDOW, DECK, PORCH, FRONT STOOP, SIT SPOT, OR MEADOW

Where can you feel the vastness of the Night sky and let your mind drift? Pick your spot! It doesn't matter where your place is—what's important is that you feel safe and can turn off any electric lights in your immediate vicinity. (Trust me, Firefly, the Night has a different energy without those buzzy little lights. I want you to have a chance to experience this.)

It's easy to *consider* creating a nighttime perch, while not actually picking a spot in the physical world that corresponds to your mental noodling. Challenge yourself to actually find a place where you can *feel* the Night.

Remember: the Night is not simply the stretch of time after the sun goes down. The Night is the vastness, the shadows, the silence, and the stars. The Night is lit differently than the day so things might look a little distorted. (Your eyes depend on light, Firefly. When you change the quality of the light, you change what you see.) Find a place where you can leave the electric lights behind and let your eyes and mind adjust to a world that is softer and less defined, a world with mysteries in every shadow. This is the Night we are stepping into.

A POCKET COMPASS

Did you know that the earliest compasses were tools not for navigation, but for divination? That's right, Firefly, compasses were used to help people find their metaphoric way, whether that was in mapping their life choices or siting their homestead.

These original compasses were invented in ancient China, where it was discovered that an iron-bearing lodestone, hung so that it could swing freely, would always point to the Earth's poles. These early compasses existed as a map for our Night-brains long before they became an instrument of precision navigation. But even the modern compass has high metaphoric value: it guides you home, especially when the world is dark. When the sun is sleeping and can't help you determine east from west, you can use a compass to find your way. You'll learn to employ a compass in more depth during your second semester.

But compasses also serve a secondary purpose: the presence of a compass is the best way to identify fellow Night School students. If you see something that looks like a watch fob hanging from someone's pocket, suspect a compatriot. If you're passing this person on the street or on the way in or out of your favorite coffee shop, the proper protocol is to half smile with the right side of your mouth and nod your head in greeting.

Please acquire a pocket compass as soon as possible after matriculation. The aesthetics of your compass are wholly up to you, but like your journal, this is a tool that will be vital for you on both the physical and metaphoric planes. If you knew your compass was going to travel with you into your dreams, what would you want it to look like?

ADDITIONAL SUPPLIES FOR SEMESTER 1

Salt

The world is full of salt, and every mystic who's ever lived has used it at one point or another. (Yes, I feel safe making that claim, Firefly, but thank you for being alert to hyperbole. While I may not know every mystic who has ever lived, I do know that, in the world of the Night, salt is as much a symbol as it is a mineral. You'll learn more about salt later in the semester.)

Salt is one of the oldest tools of the trade. There's pink, there's gray, there's Celtic and Dead Sea. It's all the same, and it's all different. Choose whatever appeals to you most to start with. I'm a huge fan of using whatever's in your cupboard. Over time you can compare, contrast, and become a connoisseur.

ADDITIONAL SUPPLIES FOR SEMESTER 2

A Rattle

Or, I should say, something that rattles. It can be an actual rattle or something rattley like dried beans, or rice, or paper clips in a mason jar.

A Pendulum

You can use a pendulum designed specifically for dowsing, or substitute in any small bob that you can hang on a string or chain—for example, a button on a thread, a key on a cord, or a bolt on a string. A necklace with a charm or ring hanging from it can also work beautifully for our purposes. (Fun fact: women used to hang their wedding ring on a chain so they could use it as a pendulum to divine the sex of their yet-to-be-born babies.)

An Herb Bundle

You'll need a bundle of dried and burnable plant material. But don't plan to burn just anything: simply because plants are natural doesn't mean they're nontoxic. Cedar, pine, juniper, myrtle, bay, lavender, sage, mugwort, and rosemary are traditional choices. Be mindful of where you're sourcing your herbs, and consider both their environmental impact and traditional relationship to other cultures, Firefly—we want to honor both the Earth and one another in our choices. You'll also want something fireproof to hold beneath your plant bundle to catch the ashes. Your bundle should be two to four inches long, a half inch to an inch wide, and loosely packed, so that oxygen, which is necessary for fire, can circulate. Bigger, in this case, is not better.

A Tarot or Oracle Deck

Chose a tarot or oracle deck simply because you like the pictures. The images should taste like ambrosia to your imagination. At the Night School, we will use the deck primarily for the illustrations, so if you don't have a deck, you can easily use other sources of imagery—like the illustrations on the pages of a book or photos you've cut from a magazine or printed from the internet.

A Scrying Mirror

A scrying mirror is simply a reflective surface. If you want to get fancy, you can use a crystal or obsidian ball, or you can choose from any number of other reflective items:

* a mirror
* polished brass

* water in a bowl
* glass (even window glass!)

Water in a metal bowl works very well for our purposes and is my favorite go-to for speaking with my Great-Aunt Helen, who's been quite dead for decades. (Which is exactly the point of scrying, Firefly: it lets you see around time's corners so the past and future are only a reflection, or a refraction, away.)

Ingredients for Bananas Foster

Don't buy these now: they'll spoil before you need them. I'll remind you and put a full list of ingredients in the welcome materials before the class begins.

An Ephemeris

An ephemeris is a table—the kind on paper, not the kind with four legs—showing the positions of celestial objects over time. While these were laboriously produced in ancient times, today you can simply download one to your phone or computer.

The word *ephemeris* comes from the Latin word meaning "diary." So essentially an ephemeris is a diary of the stars. Romantic, no?

Ephemerides (that's the plural, because Latin) have been used historically by navigators, astronomers, and astrologers. And, during the second semester of the Night School, by you.

You can find an ephemeris that is only for a month, or you can find one for the entire year. It doesn't matter which you choose, as long as you have an ephemeris specific to the months in which you are taking the Harnessing the Celestial Tides course. You might want to hold off on getting this immediately as you can easily download what you need when the time comes.

A Star Map

When we talk about the sign of Leo or Libra, we're talking about actual stars in the actual sky. I know you know that, but can you pick those stars out when you gaze at the heavens? Do you know the mythology behind each constellation? It's time to learn!

Get yourself a star map that includes the Western zodiac signs. Then, look up and start cataloging what you see.

Other Tools of Choice

During your Divination Lab, you'll be learning about various tools of the mystic. The supplies listed above will allow you to do all your coursework as well as the lab experiments. After you have divined your way through the labs, you'll have a better idea of what your own particular brand of magic is.

At that point, you may want to choose one or two mystical tools that will be your go-to implements. Once you know which types of divination you prefer, it's worth investing in instruments that are truly special. While you can learn to play on any guitar, as you advance, you'll begin to notice that the timbre of the vibrations vary amongst the different woods used for a guitar's body and that the action of the strings against the fretboard can influence your enjoyment. You'll begin to want a guitar that nestles into the curve of your waist and feels sinuous beneath your fingertips. Mystical tools are much the same: you'll want tools that suit your hands and feed your magic.

But you won't know which divination tools sing to your soul until you've experimented with the possible choices, so hold off on making any decisions until you've completed Divining the Night at the end of the first semester.

That's it, Firefly! Gather what you need and remember it doesn't have to be gorgeous or gilded. It just has to make your hands tingle with anticipation.

New Student Orientation

IS IT TIME TO BEGIN?

Has Night fallen where you are, Firefly? If it's not full dark, has the sun at least dipped below the brow of the horizon?

If not, it's not yet time for you to begin your Night School Orientation. Close your book and come back and join me when the final pinks of day have faded from the sky. I'll be right here waiting for you.

NOW, LET'S STEP INTO THE NIGHT

What do you see when you step into the Night, Firefly? When the light of the sun is removed, what remains? Are the trees in your yard limned in silver? Is your garden made of moonbeams? Are cars racing down the roads like shooting stars? Soften your gaze and let the magic in.

As I sit in my office typing this, the new moon has risen, a small dot in the upper corner of my office window, a barely seen portal against the dark sky. My tea has long since gone cold, but before I make a fresh pot, I want to get these words down for you. They are Night words and they crave this velvety void, the freshness that comes in the wake of a New Moon. They whisper both *wake up* and *dream*.

But before we slide into the Night's enigmatic embrace, let's revisit the basics:

The Night encompasses, on average, between eight and 12 hours of every 24-hour period. The exact length of the Night will vary, of course, depending on the time of year and where, exactly, you live on this ever-rotating sky sphere. What remains consistent is the simple fact that, during the midnight hours when the outer world retreats and the inner world awakes, most of us are, quite literally, unconscious. Bringing consciousness to these inward hours, and watering the magic and mystery that bloom there, is the work of the mystic and the purpose of the Night School.

Once you activate your Night-sight, you'll be able to use it by the light of day, but it is infinitely easier to step into the mysteries for the first time during the hours of darkness. The Night cradles your secrets, keeping them safe like treasured wool sweaters in a cedar trunk, then it gently unfolds them for you to try on. (The day forgets to be sweet and soothing: it will accost you with your own truths and want you to thank it for the bruises of enlightenment.)

So pull a blanket round your shoulders and let your daylight world fall away. See if you can remember who you are and who you want to be. Refinding life's magic is our journey for the next two semesters, and this is our quiet time together before we begin; our time to let the Night soften us so we can slip sideways through its portals and learn something unexpected and potent.

We begin with getting to know the Night. Not the words *the night* or the concept of "the night," but the actual sueded darkness of Night. The one that exists right outside your door, Firefly.

Finish your cocoa and grab your coat. It's time to go outside (yes, even if it's chilly): to begin to step into the Night you need to stand under the starlight and breathe it in.

Slowly unleash your senses:

Focus on your sense of sight. Observe the Night's landscape without judgment, noticing what you see and what you don't. What stands out to you? (And what doesn't?) What (or who) catches your attention? How do familiar things look once they are shrouded in darkness?

What does the Night sound like? Focus less on cars driving by or your neighbor's dog barking and more on what exists in the sliver of starlight in between . . . Try opening your eyes and closing them. Does this change what you hear? If the Night were a song, what song would it be? Do you hear creatures? Are they on the ground? In the sky? In a tree? Can you tell just based on what you hear, or is sound itself fluid and strange in the blackness of Night?

How does the Night feel on your skin? Is it a blanket or a butterfly kiss? Is the Night air humid, playful, sensuous, chilly?

Now use your nose. What do you smell standing under the Night sky? (Is it strange to be sniffing the Night? How does it feel for you, Firefly?)

Open your mouth and taste the Night. Yes, it will feel . . . unusual. Do it anyway. Let the Night wrap around your tongue so you can savor the notes of menthol and mystery.

Finally, open yourself fully to the Night, allowing all your senses to sing simultaneously. Like a crisp apple, there is sweetness and crunch, a cool tartness, a breaking of the skin. Breathe into it. Gently notice how your Nighttime knowings differ from the knowings of your daytime self.

Now, return to the cosmic question: *Who are you in the Night?*

Your Night-self is the mirror image of your daylight self; it exists in balance, as necessary in forming who you are as the very oxygen you breathe. Light cannot exist without dark and we, too, must have this balance within us to be whole. Getting to know the shimmer of your Night-persona, with her inner gaze and outer knowing, is vital in the original sense of the word: it brings *vita*, life.

In your heart, reach out to the Night. Ask what it has to share with you. Pay careful, but soft, attention to its reply. Practice observing and noticing. Remember, you're not deciding whether these noticings are good or bad, you're just letting them land like snowflakes on your winter mittens.

When you're ready, head back indoors. Make yourself a fresh cup of something soothing. I have a little homework for you before you head off to dreaming.

And, yes, Firefly, you need sleep and dreams. While the Night cracks open your mind and heart in ways the day does not, while it brings with it whispers of magic and mystery, it is also meant to be a time for rest. Through your Night School studies you'll learn to open your consciousness to these subconscious hours, but that doesn't mean your studies should make you disregard your circadian rhythms. Recent studies have shown that your brain detoxes while you're sleeping, so keep your mind clean and be sure to get some zzz's.

But before you turn the lights out, let's have some fun!

HOMEWORK

Get into school mode with your very first homework assignment.

Ready to wade in?

(Don't worry: the water's warm, scented with night-blooming jasmine, and dappled with starlight.)

Night Haiku

Gather your observations from your time outdoors so you can write a Night Haiku. You may remember from literature classes that a haiku is a type of short-form poem only three lines long, which originated in 13th-century Japan. They're often about nature, so an ode to Nighttime is fairly traditional fodder.

Start by thinking of a few words you can use to describe the smelled, tasted, and heard sensations of the Night.

Sometimes it's hard to match language to sensation, and the relationship between words and feelings can be tenuous. Let this space between lived experience and language feel like freedom—the perfect excuse to string your words together in unexpected ways in order to create unexplored meanings. Words that would never sit side by side during the day are perfectly comfortable cohabitating during the Night:

> *poke and perfection*
>
> *mercury and miasma*
>
> *needle and dreams*

Remember, a haiku is three lines long. And although the lines don't need to rhyme, you do have to count the syllables:

* **Five for the first line**
* **Seven for the second**
* **Five for the third.**

So a haiku looks like this:

> *Into the falling*
>
> *needles of Night, perfect stars*
>
> *poke holes in the dark.*

Or

> *Hush, green frog burping*
>
> *In the miasma. Owl will*
>
> *ruin your dreaming.*

Or even

> *Mercury rose fast,*
>
> *a flaming needle, streaking*
>
> *through velvet sky dreams.*

Your turn, Firefly.

Write a haiku or two describing the Night, then inscribe your verse, as well as notes on your observations from your trip outside, in your journal. Easy-peasy.

Night Collage

Images resonate within us in a different way than words do. They crack open the door into the land of symbolism and iconography, which we will be working with during your first semester at the Night School.

Begin to play with images by creating a collage. Start by gathering photos and illustrations that evoke the sensations you felt as you stepped into the Night. Jumble them about and juxtapose them in various ways, exploring the combinations of color and symbolism to signify sensation.

This homework assignment is not meant to be completed in a single evening. Tonight, make a start by looking at images. Over the weeks to come you can select the ones that speak to you and begin to arrange your creation.

Allow yourself full freedom as you cut out Night images from a magazine and paste them into your journal, or use an online collaging app to create a mood board of the Night. You may find there are pictures that evoke the Night for you, but don't have what you might think of as a "Night look." For example, a photo of a damp spiderweb gleaming in sunlight may evoke something within you that feels of the Night, but obviously, the image was taken in the daylight. You're looking for symbols and signposts that evoke the *sensations* of the Night, not for images taken at Night, so absolutely include whatever photos, signs, glyphs, doodles, and even objects that bring you into alignment with the Night's energy.

How and where you arrange your collage is completely up to your own creative instincts. (Yes, you have creative instincts. If they've been dormant, consider this their invitation to poke their heads once more from the inner recesses of your being.) You could tape images to a window in your living room or to the mirror in your bathroom. You could use a table-top as your canvas and arrange images and objects upon it. You could use paint or markers or colored pencils. Add words or the first fronds of a fern your fingers found when you were feeling into the Night. Perhaps your collage will be swaths of color, which relate to what you tasted on the Night air, or glyphs you've created to mimic the way the clouds moved against the moon.

See what happens if you approach this project with no expectations.

What might you create if the only reason for this collage to exist were to support your dreams and creativity? If you knew that this would be your Night's nest, a place to let your mind rest and bed down, what would you desire?

This collage might be the work of months, a growing, evolving experi-ence of the hours between dusk and dawn that you can return to in the day-time to help you remember the feeling of the Night and who you become in its embrace. Remember: this is just for fun and just for you, Firefly, so don't worry about what Ms. Atwood said about your artwork in second grade.

Extra Credit

If you're used to watching TV or being on the computer in the evening and need some nonelectronic activities to replace your screen time, try read-ing Basho's traditional haiku (his frog poems are significantly better than mine!) or Natalie Goldberg's exploration of Japan and the haiku form in her book *Three Simple Lines.*

A final note:

As you move into your first semester of the Night School, remember to read your lessons through the eyes of this Nighttime self you're discover-ing. Softness and wonder will bring the lessons of the Night alive.

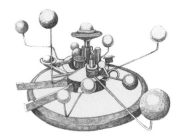

YOUR COURSE SCHEDULE

You have been preregistered for a roster of the 101-level classes, which are required for all Night School students.

While your courses are prescribed, you have choices about how you'll engage with your studies. You can take a linear approach and handle your classes sequentially, allowing each course to build conceptually upon the one before. Alternately, you can engage with all of the semester's classes simultaneously, rotating through the courses in a circular pattern, so that you are doing one lesson from each every week.

And then there's the option of hopping about like Basho's frog, taking classes as the mood strikes you. This will work best if you're already familiar with the contours of the mystic and the landscape of the Night. For novitiates, stick with the previously discussed methods.

Whichever path you choose, take the time to digest one lesson before snacking on the next.

TRACKING YOUR PROGRESS

Don't you just love crossing things off your to-do list, Firefly?

(I have to admit, sometimes I add easy things to the list simply so I can cross them off: *brush teeth CHECK!*)

Here at the Night School, we mark lessons complete in one of two ways: you can either put a star next to the finished class or, at the bottom of the page, note the glyph for the moon's phase on the Night you completed the lesson. Be sure to pause and congratulate yourself as you add your finishing glyph. Gold star—or moon, as the case might be!

At the Night School, we do essay-style exams at the end of your second semester. The point of the exam is to help you weave together the threads you've pulled from your various courses. Are you allowed to read the prompt early? Is that cheating? Good question, Firefly.

If this were a day school, there'd be a concrete answer.

But this is the Night School, where we subscribe to a flowier version of time than is generally accepted in the light of day. If Nighttime is nonlinear, then there's a good chance you've already seen the final exam question. And so, the issue of when, in linear terms, you see the test is irrelevant. Thus, we can postulate that there's no such thing as cheating on your Night School lessons or exams. *Phew!*

While there are no rules, I do highly recommend multiple cups of tea, time spent staring at the moon's shadow, and many hot baths by candlelight as you dance your way through the Night School curriculum.

The courses require you to dig deep, sharpen your curiosity, and use your emotional and spiritual intelligence to discover new truths and different ways of being.

So . . . are you ready to take a peek behind life's curtain?

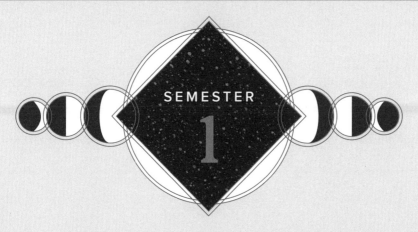

IT'S THE FIRST NIGHT OF SCHOOL, FIREFLY.

I'm sure you've already studied your course schedule, but I wanted to take a moment to walk you through the semester and let you know why each class has been chosen especially for you.

You'll be starting in Midnight Foundations (Philosophy 101). This is a required course for all Night School students. Whether you're just getting started or have spent decades studying a spiritual, mystical, or healing tradition, you'll glean inspiration, as well as a sense of history and rootedness, from exploring the principles covered in here.

After Midnight Foundations, you'll travel inward with the Mysteries of Being Human. Give yourself space for this course: the inward journey can be challenging. But when you discover, deep in the caverns of your inner being, the purring dragon of your personal power, it all becomes magically worthwhile.

While the day runs on coffee and doughnuts, the Night runs on tendrils of pure mystical energy. You'll explore these tendrils in Divining the Night where you'll learn the Night School's unique take on the long-practiced art of divination. First the theory, then the fun: you'll get to the Lab for Divining the Night in Semester 2.

Now, allow the lights to dim and your intuition to bubble up. Open your mind and carry your compass: the darkness awaits!

Note that you'll often have a small homework assignment with each lesson. Complete these explorations of your Night-self in your journal within 72 hours of finishing the lesson.

Remember to track your progress with a star or the glyph for the moon's phase in the lower corner of the page. (And then give yourself a high five and a cup of cocoa!)

Lesson 1:

EVERYTHING HOLDS A SPARK OF ENERGY

In both animals and humans, scientists have observed the spark that occurs when sperm meets egg. This spark of creation is like a personal Big Bang moment for every being on the planet.

Let's take this concept one step further, Firefly, and posit that *every-thing* holds the creative energy of its own beginning. (Your day-brain doesn't have to agree with this hypothesis. If it's protesting, simply relax your mind and allow the metaphors and magic of the Night to infuse your consciousness.)

It's easy to understand the concept of a spark of initiative energy when we look at a baby or a work of art. It's harder to find that spark in mass-produced objects. But it's there. Can you think of an inanimate object that has felt alive to you? Maybe it was your first car, which you called by name, or your old computer, which only turned on when you sweet-talked it.

Looking for the spark makes it easy to find magic in all the facets of your daily life. The world becomes animated and alive.

Homework: What Feels Alive?

Look around you right at this moment. What feels alive to you? What doesn't? Why? It's time to examine your preconceptions, Firefly!

Choose something that feels plastic-y and inanimate. Now, in your imagination, trace its story all the way back to the beginnings. Imagine the process by which it was conceived and made. Allow your eyes to open to all the creative energy behind this object. How many people put a little bit of themselves into its creation? Can you find its spark?

Next time you eat a vegetable, repeat this same process. Mentally trace it all the way back to its origin, to the moment you can imagine a farmer with strong hands and sunbaked skin sowing the seed of the plant that will grow until it eventually produces the very food you are now eating.

How do you feel when you think about and acknowledge the spark of creation within the things you encounter throughout your evening? Do you feel more connected to the world around you? Does the landscape of your living room feel a bit more animated? Maybe you're sitting on a sofa whose frame was constructed from wood that grew tall in the forests of Alaska and whose fabric is the marriage of sheep's wool from Uzbekistan and cotton grown in Iowa. All those beginnings—the tree, the sheep, the cotton—have an energy. And so does the sofa itself, dreamed up by a designer and made by human hands. Sitting on the sofa, enjoying a night-cap and a spot of TV suddenly becomes a trippy experience!

Relax into it, and remember: the Night has a logic all its own.

Lesson 2:

ONE ALWAYS MANAGES TO BECOME TWO

Let's look more closely at the creative spark we discussed last Night, Firefly.

Stories from around the globe tell us what happened "in the beginning." Remember, "in the beginning" is the moment when the spark of creation zings something new into existence.

In the beginning God created the heaven and the earth.

And the earth was without form, and void; and darkness was upon the face of the deep. And the Spirit
of God moved upon the face of the waters.

And God said, Let there be light: and there was light.

And God saw the light, that it was good: and God
divided the light from the darkness.

And God called the light Day, and the darkness he called
Night. And the evening and the morning were the
first day.

—The Old Testament of the Bible

The Tao that can be told of
Is not the Absolute Tao;
The Names that can be given
Are not Absolute Names.
The Nameless is the origin of Heaven and Earth;
The Named is the Mother of All Things.

—Tao Te Ching

Avalokiteshvara Bodhisattva practicing profound Prajna Paramita
clearly saw the five skandhas to be empty transcending all suf-
fering and difficulties.
Sariputra!
Form is empty therefore no difficulties are to be discerned.
Feeling is empty therefore no feeling.
Thought is empty therefore no knowing.
Volition is empty therefore no doing.
Consciousness is empty therefore no awakening.
Why is this?
Sariputra!
Without form there is no emptiness.
Without emptiness there is no form.
Form is then emptiness. Emptiness is then form.
Feeling, thought, volition and consciousness are also like this.

—The Heart Sutra

Then, some time later, she became pregnant, this one who stood
upon the Earth. And then, when her term had come, one male child
was born the right way; he was born the way a person should be
born. But the other one was in such a hurry out that he came out
right through her body; he killed their mother. . . . The way they
were, they had different kinds of minds. And now whatever this
Thaluhyawaku would think of doing, Tawiskala would change it to
the opposite way.

—from a transcribed and translated oral telling by
Demus Elm, translated by Floyd G. Lounsbury and
Bryan Gick, The Oneida Creation Story,
University of Nebraska Press, Lincoln, NE (2000)

These are just a few of the many early origin stories of one becoming two. We call this phenomenon duality. Duality is how we begin to differentiate various aspects of our reality so we can understand the world around us. (And it leads to important questions like which came first: the chicken or the egg? These are questions that the day-brain will never satisfactorily answer. But the Night-mind? That's another story!)

Note: duality is a beginning point, Firefly. None of these creation stories *ended* with one becoming two. The world is multifaceted and beautifully (and mysteriously!) varied. Understanding the concept of duality lets us begin to put some points on the graph paper of the universe so we can then find the many ways in which those points can be connected.

Homework: Go Dark

In our modern world, we use electric lights to ease the duality between day and Night. Most of us have forgotten the flavor of true darkness. Lights and electronics glow through the Night, obscuring the stars. But by buffering ourselves from the darkness, we're losing the tension of duality. When the lights are all lit, the Night isn't that much different from the day. Turn out the lights so the Night can become its true self.

(This is also the best exercise you can use to invite your Night-self to make an appearance, Firefly.)

Choose a time to go dark. Turn off all electronics, and don't use a flashlight or electric lamp. If you have streetlights near your windows, draw the curtains. Use candlelight or battery-operated tea lights to keep the lighting soft. The flickering glow of candles is a very different sort of illumination than the steady luminescence of a lamp. This softer light hits your eyes and your brain in unexpected ways, like the difference between flat water and seltzer.

Do your thoughts change when you're in true dark? Do the things you're willing to discuss with your partner or family shift? Does your writing flow in a different way? Do you desire different books or drinks or ways of sitting? In the dark, can you relinquish your daylight persona and rewrite the rules of being yourself?

SCIENCE AND MAGIC ARE TWO SIDES OF THE SAME COIN

When we contemplate the universe with our eyes closed, we realize that there is no great rift between science and spirituality. In fact, these two ways of understanding the world have been braided together through the ages, Firefly.

In our last lesson, we looked at religious, mythical, and spiritual creation myths. Now let's look at science's creation story. It's called the Big Bang Theory and it essentially goes like this:

> About 13.82 billion years ago, all that is was a singular void. That void imploded, scattering bits of itself outward in ever expanding waves. At first this new universe was dense and there was no light. But after about 380,000 years, the expansion allowed for the creation of neutral atoms, which let light come into the darkness.

When you use your daylight mind, this story is vastly different from the cultural tales of the last lesson. But when you soften your gaze and peer round the edges of things, science and myth are rather synonymous: they both say, "in the beginning there was nothingness which somehow or other divided into darkness and light."

It turns out that a lot of what we think of as magical can be explained by science, Firefly. For instance, people have been taking elderberry syrup for the flu since forever ago. Some people (still!) think this is simply magical thinking. But a researcher at Tel Aviv University discovered the mechanism by which this herbal medicine works: flu viruses are shaped like medieval maces, all pokey and pointy. Those points are meant to puncture the human cell wall so the virus can get in. But elderberry puts a glob on the tip of each of the virus's spikes so it can't penetrate and infect the cell. Magical? Yes. Scientific? You betcha.

For fun, let's take this concept one step further. (Remember, Firefly, this is the Night—not only are you allowed, you're encouraged to poke around the edges of reality.) Many religions and cultures have long believed that a well-trained mystic can be in one place and send a bit of their spirit somewhere else. This is called bilocation. The secondary appearance of the mystic is sometimes called a doppelgänger. The Christian mystic Isidore the Farmer was said to be seen simultaneously plowing the fields and attending mass; a number of modern Hindu gurus including Neem Karoli Baba and Lahiri Mahasaya are also said to be able to bilocate. If you dig into the literature, Firefly, you'll find hints about bilocation in stories from the Sufis to the Jewish mystics to various indigenous cultures across the globe.

From a standard scientific perspective, this might sound like pure fiction. Except that experiments at Stanford University have shown that quarks, as well as atoms and photons, can be in multiple places at the same time—it's called quantum mechanics, and it is truly mind-boggling. Is it so hard to believe that your spirit might be made of quarks or photons or atoms that have this two-places-at-once superpower?

Homework: Dreaming on Dualities

This brings us to the big question: what if science and myth are not a duality but instead two ways of expressing the same concepts? What would happen if you believed you could explore an idea either through scientific thinking or magical thinking and get the same result? For your homework, think on this notion:

Science is simply daytime's version of Nighttime magic.

When you curl up in your bed to go to sleep tonight, set your intention to consult your dreams and see if they concur.

ALCHEMY AND LAUNDRY HAVE A LOT IN COMMON

Let's talk alchemy.

Alchemy is an ancient science that can support your soul work by helping you untangle thoughts and emotions that are keeping you stuck. The concepts of alchemy are foundational to mysticism so we will be exploring them in glorious depth during your second semester. For now, let's keep it simple:

The basic steps of an alchemical experiment are *separate, purify,* and *put it all back together again.* Think of this process like doing laundry: first you separate the lights from the darks, then you give everything a good wash, and finally you fold and put everything back in your closet. This alchemical step-by-step process is incredibly useful for sorting everyday dilemmas.

(1) THE FIRST STEP IS SEPARATE: **When the threads that make up an issue in your life are bound together, it's hard to truly understand the problem and easy to become reactive. To separate the component parts of the problem into manageable pieces, put your tangled thoughts in the middle of a Mind Map, then tease out the individual strands. Just like sorting the laundry, things will feel less jumbled once they're in color-coded piles! This will help you gain clarity on the specifics of your thoughts and feelings.**

What, you might be wondering, do I mean by *teasing out the individual strands*?

Let's look at an example together.

Say your central concern is that you want to be a forest ranger, but your family is pushing you to become a brain surgeon. One strand of this issue might be that you're angry at your mother for not seeing you as you see yourself. (This is a very common strand, Firefly.) Another strand might be that you're close with your grandparents and your family is concerned about you moving away from them. Maybe a third is that you dread wearing a uniform every day, but don't want to admit it. Each strand of the larger issue—that you want to be a forest ranger but your family wants you to get a medical degree—can be explicated on your Mind Map.

Never heard of a *Mind Map*, Firefly? They look like this:

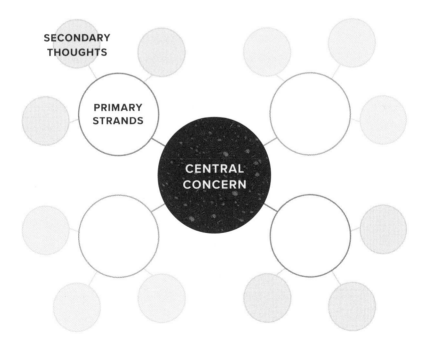

(2) PURIFY: If you were actually doing laundry, this would be when you'd throw your clothes in the washing machine. In our alchemical problem-solving process, this is the stage at which you work with each individual strand of thought or emotion to clear it and find resolution within yourself.

Working to heal an individual strand might involve things like:

* Writing a letter to the people involved—remembering that the "people involved" might just be the many sides of your own personality! After you write the letter, burn it. Allow the burning to symbolize *release*. That might be releasing other people's hold on your emotions or releasing yourself from unrealistic expectations or from conflicting thoughts.

* You could also consider writing a letter that you actually send. This simple act opens the door to further conversation. Note that I said *letter* not *email*. The surprise of receiving a piece of paper and a stamp will get you a more thoughtful response than an electronic transmission.

* Perhaps you take yourself to therapy or to see someone trained in spiritual reconciliation, like a counselor affiliated with your religious faith or a person trained in neo-shamanism, to help you resolve restricting thought patterns.

* Consider utilizing your own subconscious: before you go to sleep, set the intention to work through this knotty problem in your dreams.

These ideas are meant to inspire you to find a starting point for the process of exploring and healing through alchemical purification. Get creative, Firefly! The Night mind works through metaphor so consider other ways you can symbolize cleansing and releasing.

The Purification step might be the work of minutes or months. The amount of time it's going to take will depend on what you reveal to yourself through your Mind Mapping and how much attention each strand you've discovered requires. You may need help to tie off or cut some strands. That's okay. You're making progress simply by doing this work. Don't get all judgy with yourself if you need a therapist or acupuncturist or good friend to help you through!

(3) BRING IT ALL BACK TOGETHER: **Why?** Because everything is interconnected, Firefly. After you've unbraided the threads and purified each one, do some journaling to examine the patterns that emerged through the process. For instance, if you've realized in the above example that your mom does love you but just has a different idea about what's right for your life, you can stop taking her behavior personally. Purification changes how you see things. So once you purify, reexamine the original issue. Now that your thoughts aren't tangled, you will see the root of your problem more clearly. Maybe you initially thought you'd simply stop talking to your mom in order to feel free to do what you want with your life; post-purification you might decide to have an honest conversation with her, knowing that your mom's love for you will win her over in the end.

It's Step 3 that is often neglected, Firefly, which is a shame because Step 3 is where the gold of this emotional process lies! In Step 3 you discover the holy grail of alchemy: the moment when everything that was disparate becomes integrated. . . . Just like when you return your laundered clothes neatly to your closet.

Homework: Do Your Laundry!

Choose one problem in your life that you're ready to work on. Follow the alchemical process to bring light into your shadowed spaces.

Chances are you won't be able to do this entire process in just one Night, so allow yourself time. You can make that time mystically meaningful by designating the length of a moon cycle or the number of days that a butterfly spends in its cocoon as your temporal container for doing this work. (I don't know how many days it takes a caterpillar to go through metamorphosis, Firefly, so if you want the answer to that question, you can add researching it to your homework assignment!)

Lesson 5:

CHANGE IS THE ONLY CONSTANT

Change is the only constant, Firefly.

Heraclitus, an ancient Greek philosopher, noted that you can't step in the same river twice.

Why? Because you change and the river changes.

Let's look at this idea a little more closely. Say you're about to step into a powerful waterway, like the Nile. Let's even say that you, being an intrepid adventurer fond of the alluvial mysteries, have visited this particular riverbank before. Let's go one step further and speculate that the stars are in the exact same place on the horizon and the same palm trees are sighing in a gentle breeze, just like they were the last time you dipped a toe into this mighty river. In your mind, you're returning. It's been a pilgrimage to get here, and now you once again stand on the Nile's banks.

You believe you're stepping into the same river.

But are you?

The water molecules that caressed your ankles when you last visited have long since sped out to sea. The exact particles of silt that squished between your toes are probably now part of the seabed of the Mediterranean, possibly miles from where you currently stand. Even though your

come in making it so. The second acknowledges our limited vision and leaves space for outcomes even better than what our Nighttime self could dream up.

Tip #2

Now that you have an intention that's well thought out—and complete with a phrase to cover your pajama-clad derriere—you'll want to recommit to this intention every evening. Just because energy follows intention doesn't mean it follows it immediately! Time is a tricksy thing, Firefly. So each Night, before you go to sleep, speak your intention out loud and listen for anything that rings false or feels incomplete so that you can correct your course.

Note that many old magics follow the rule of three: meaning you repeat your intention three times. This is a failsafe, so that if you accidentally shout in a moment of anger: "You silly woman! I wish that sausage was stuck to your nose!" the universe will simply hold its breath and wait to see if you repeat your request.

Phew! This is a lot of information to slurp down in one evening, Firefly! Your only homework is to dream and digest. We'll pick this up tomorrow Night.

Lesson 7:

ENERGY FOLLOWS INTENTION, PART 2

How's that spoonful of intention-setting syrup sitting with you, Firefly? Did you fall asleep fantasizing about buying a new car or hiring a live-in chef to cook your every meal? Let's continue our lessons so you can make whatever you're dreaming into a reality!

We started last Night discussing how energy follows intention and wrapped up with various ways to be deliberate and complete with your intending. Let's pick up our list at tip 3.

Tip #3

One thing that's often neglected in intention setting is checking for preexisting roadblocks that stand between you and your intention. What might these be?

* Your own negative self-talk
* Fear
* Jealousy
* Old thought patterns
* Lack of money or other resources

While you might not be able to immediately change your physical circumstances, you can let go of the energetic imprint those circumstances have created in a myriad of ways. Below, I'm going to give you two good options. Use my suggestions as jumping-off points to create your own situation-specific rituals of release. Remember *energy follows intention.* That means each of these rituals is really about the intention you use to fuel it. So if you want to do a slow striptease under the stars as you envision your burdens falling away with your clothes, that could very well get the job done. Or if you're lucky enough to live by the ocean, you could whisper what you're scared of into a conch and cast the shell, and your fears, out to sea. But usually, Firefly, you won't have time for a complex ritual and will want an easy, tried-and-true solution:

Write and Burn

On a piece of paper write down everything you see as an obstacle. Be sure to add a nice catchall phrase like "this and anything else that I am currently unaware of." Then burn the paper, letting all the emotions that don't serve you go up in smoke.

Give It a Salting

Take a handful of salt. Imagine the salt is a giant magnet pulling all the emotional obstacles to the surface of your hands. (This makes complete sense when you use your Night brain, Firefly.) Scrub and rinse your hands, picturing all that negativity washing down the drain with the salt. *Ahhhhhh,* isn't that a relief?

Tip #4

Remember when I said an intention is a wish with some oomph behind it? Wishes, when not magically super-charged, are like dandelion seeds— light and fluffy. An intention is what happens when that seed takes root, anchoring itself in the ground as it sends out tendrils to look for water and nutrients.

Your intention needs to be fed. It's hungry for your attention and action. There's an old cartoon of a man praying. His prayer is "Please let me win the lottery, God!" God's reply is "Help me out: buy a ticket!"

Help your intention out. Once you set your clear intention, choose three action steps to help it manifest. Then do them.

Tip #5

Picture in your mind that what you intend has already happened. This is called visualization. So if you intend to find your perfect life partner, picture waking up next to them. How would your day look and feel different? What texts would you send them in the middle of the day? What would they be doing in the evening while you are sitting reading *The Night School* by candlelight?

Remember how we talked about science and magic representing two sides of the same coin? If your daylight brain rebels against all this woo-woo, pop "science + visualization and healing" into your search engine.... Boom! Any questions?

BALANCE IS FOUND IN
UNDERSTANDING OPPOSITES

Balance is found in understanding opposites, Firefly, and, by understanding them, being able to shift away from the extremes and come to center.

You may think that the middle ground is milquetoast. You may even fear that coming to a philosophical center means you're abdicating some important bit of your free will. If you've ever refused to budge from your ideals because moving even a millimeter off your chosen position "will compromise my morals!" you know exactly what I'm talking about. But working with, rather than against, polarities allows us to achieve balance—which is *not* the same as blandness! The dynamic tension of opposition invigorates both polarities: day is better when paired with Night, summer is always dreaming of winter, and yin knows it will someday be yang.

With this understanding we can see that opposition causes some big pendulum swings. Day and Night are quite different from one another, and neither is sustainable alone. Isn't it interesting that the old tales tell us that in Fairyland it is always twilight, the time between day and Night? Dusk and dawn are the two times within a 24-hour period when there is balance, Firefly.

There is a quiet magic in this balance. If, as a child, you and a friend ever tried to offset a teeter-totter—each of you wriggling and squiggling until you reached that perfect (and fleeting!) moment when you both hung in the air unmoving—you know this magic. Even if your head doesn't remember, the place in the middle of your gut, the part of you that wriggled and jiggled, can recall the magical feel of achieving equilibrium.

Ideas will also move between polarities, and just as with physical bodies, the stable place exists smack in the middle. Have you ever gone on an ice cream

1. FIND A PLACE TO BUILD YOUR ALTAR. Don't just plunk it down on the first surface you come across, Firefly. Your altar is a sacred workspace. Where will it be out of the reach of prying hands, but still easily accessible to you each evening? Keep in mind that your altar will be in active use. It may not always look pretty so don't think of it as home decor!

2. ONCE YOU HAVE CHOSEN YOUR SPACE, CLEAN IT OFF. Maybe that means a scrub with soap and water, or maybe you want to burn herbs or incense to cleanse the energy (more on this in your next course!). The idea is to achieve energetic neutrality before you add things to your altar.

3. NOW YOU'RE READY TO ADD OBJECTS TO YOUR ALTAR. Because this particular altar space is meant to be a microcosm of the larger world, a fabulous way to begin is to reflect on the season you are currently in. If it's winter, think about what you would place on your altar to create a small-scale version of what's going on outside your window. How would you represent the cold? The wind? What shapes and colors are you seeing outside, and how can you signify them on your altar? Next add objects to represent the people in your life. Consider what else is important to you: your work? A social cause? Your animals?

4. REMEMBER THIS IS *YOUR* SACRED WORK SPACE: the objects you choose only have to have meaning for *you*. In fact, when you choose objects because you think you're supposed to or that they're "what goes on an altar" they often detract from the greater whole you're creating.

Once your altar is built, give it a good look over. How did you arrange things? Which objects are near one another and which are well spaced? Is it symmetrical or asymmetrical? Your altar is a mirror. What additional information is it showing to you?

Lesson 11:

THE LAW OF FORGETFULNESS
AND WHAT TO DO ABOUT IT

Memory is a creature of the Night. It's not a crystal clear recording device but instead a beast fueled by association and attention. So even if you think you're going to, you won't remember every symbol you've explored, every vision you've dreamed, and every archetype you've visited with. What gets encoded into your brain regarding a particular person, event, or thing is based on what you considered important at the time. Let's say you had a stomachache and made a cup of herbal tea to ease the pain. If the tea happened to ease a cramp in your left thigh, but did nothing for the stomachache, you would walk away from the experience thinking "that tea didn't work." Months later, when you again had a cramp in your left thigh, you might have a flash of "I think I made a tea for this!" but chances are you wouldn't be able to remember the ingredients, because in your mind the tea didn't work and was therefore forgettable.

This is why we write things down.

Writing breeds insights, jogs memories, and allows you to keep track of what works for you—whether it's a tip, trick, or something that feels nourishing to your Night-self.

Writing can sometimes be intimidating, but remember, your spirit doesn't care whether or not you can spell or if your sentence structure would make Mrs. Kriebel's eyeballs squish out. (You didn't have a "Mrs. Kriebel"? Insert the name of your own educational boogey-monster instead!)

So, if you haven't already, pull out your journal and start using it. You're about to launch into your next course, and you'll want to take notes on what you're gleaning from your lessons so you can return to the teachings that inspire and nurture you.

Homework: Notice Your Noticing

Let's see what your subconscious is noticing, Firefly.

Set a timer for 10 minutes and write about the world around you. All you're doing is reporting: "A squirrel just ran across a limb of the white oak . . ." and "This is boring. Why do I have to write for 10 minutes?" and "I keep thinking about roses. In my mind they have no scent and I keep burying my nose in their petals, but my fingers are cut by the thorns. . . . Huh, I wonder what that's about?"

Timed writing will help loosen the bindings on your subconscious. Repeated use of this exercise will unearth all sorts of interesting tidbits you've been storing away from your conscious mind. The subconscious is a treasure trove of intuitive knowings, and this exercise will help you gain insider access.

ADDITIONAL READINGS AND RESOURCES

Many of the ideas in this course trace their way back to the ancient Hellenistic world. Want a challenge, Firefly? Read Aristotle or Plato—or read Aristotle *and* Plato and compare the two! Marcus Aurelius's *Meditations* is approachable; Pliny the Elder's *Natural History* isn't, but it claims to hold all the knowledge of the ancient world, so it might be worth the effort. *Fragments: The Collected Wisdom of Heraclitus* by Brooks Haxton is not an exact translation of the pre-Socratic philosopher's remaining works but instead a poetic journey into their meaning—how very Night of him!

Wait! you might be thinking, *that's a long list of white men you just told me to read.* And you'd be right, Firefly. That lack of diversity can be jarring, and maybe even a little uninspiring. But let's not dismiss them simply because they're white and male—although you should absolutely dismiss them for faulty or unimaginative thinking! Most of the works of early philosophy were written by men, many of them white. Like it or not, their thoughts are a part of the foundation of intellectual and mystical thought. So do we dismiss them entirely? Or do we contextualize their thoughts?

Let's look at this as an opportunity to apply lesson 8 and consider how to find balance. What would it feel like to read these books, keeping in mind the writers' biases? Or to turn on your Night-brain and imagine the unknown lover or sister who critiqued and edited the famous philosophers over the dinner table: "See what you did here, Arty? That's a false dichotomy. How about looking at it this way?"

Luckily, some works survive that take us out of the domain of *white* men (even if we are still in the domain of *men* and in the realm of cultures that favored written history over oral). Beyond the views of the ancient Hellenistic world, you can explore the philosophies of ancient East Asian cultures. Read Lao Tzu's *Tao Te Ching* or *The Yellow Emperor's Classic of Medicine* or the Ayurvedic text *Charaka Samhita*.

EASIER ADDITIONAL READINGS AND RESOURCES

Looking for something a bit less strenuous? Research Fibonacci sequences and ask yourself how they relate to what you've been studying.

Quantum physics is tough, Firefly, but *Einstein's Dreams* by Alan Lightman makes it fun and approachable.

Want to watch the master connect the moon to a milkshake or a lantern to a peacock? Tom Robbins's book *Jitterbug Perfume* is a romp through the bizarre ways the universe interconnects with itself.

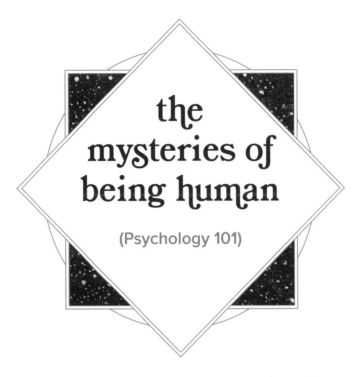

the mysteries of being human

(Psychology 101)

WELCOME TO THE MYSTERIES OF BEING HUMAN, THE KEY class to understanding the central figure in your Night-life: *you.*

Why, you might wonder, are your personal quirks, quandaries, and idiosyncrasies important to the study of mysticism?

Imagine you're out on a lake in a canoe. (It might be wooden, or metal, or made of green cheese. The material of the canoe doesn't matter for illuminating my point, so whatever you're picturing is just perfect.) The water is moonlit blue-green, and you're serenely paddling: a stroke on the left, then a stroke on the right, shifting the oar from one side of the boat to the other to keep from spinning in circles. (If you've never actually canoed, Firefly, know that paddling on each side is necessary to keep you moving forward in a somewhat straight line.) Your evening row is not a simple pleasure cruise. You're canoeing to a destination on the far side of

the lake. Over and over again, you choose a point on the opposite shore—a little house or an outcropping of stone—and you steer toward it. (This is a bit like setting your intention.) Frustratingly, you keep ending up slightly to the left of where you intend to go.

As you grow more and more annoyed, you examine your paddle and the parts of the hull you can see, searching for a defect in your equipment. But no defect can be found. It's only when you remember that *you* are also involved in this process, and realize that because you're right-handed you're inadvertently pushing your canoe to the left, that you can make the necessary adjustments to reach your target.

Until you bring yourself—the person who is both guiding the boat and doing the paddling—into the equation, you'll continue to inadvertently steer off course.

So forget everything you might have learned about staying objective in your academic studies: your thoughts and feelings are paddling along, influencing how you interact with the mystical world that you're exploring. It's essential, Firefly, that you gain at least a basic understanding of yourself in order for your magical explorations to make any sense. In many ways, you are the greatest mystery of all. There are worlds within you: your body is a miracle, your mind a treasure trove, and your heart a place of multitudinous vistas. As Jung put it: "Your visions will become clear only when you can look into your own heart. Who looks outside, dreams; who looks inside, awakes." (Letters, 1973)

In a magical worldview, you must put yourself within the workings of the universe. As you'll learn in your coming classes, your thoughts, attitudes, and beliefs will influence everything you do from dreams to divinations.

It can be fairly difficult to see yourself clearly, Firefly, and you wouldn't be the first (or the last) to consider this a daunting task. *Why are you cruel to your sister? How come you can't do math? And what's with your absolute aversion to green peas?* Most of the time it's much easier to accept ourselves than to delve into the nooks and crannies of our personalities, proclivities, and failings.

But do you really accept yourself? Or do you replay your day in the moments before sleep, reliving the fight with your sister, the embarrassing miscalculation at the grocery store, or your fury that your partner cannot remember a simple thing like not to serve you green peas?

Coming to an understanding, and a truce, with yourself is truly a lifetime's work. This course is merely a beginning . . . albeit a glorious one, full of intriguing insight!

(Okay, yes: beginnings can pinch like new shoes and burn like those torturous metal bars you're expected to sit on in your canoe. Don't worry, I'll start you with a bit of history, so you'll have time to warm to the concept of paddling about in your own psyche.)

The focus inward is the difference between this course and a daylighter's psychology class. Daylighters emphasize what's *out there*—how the people around you behave, think, and feel—while the Night School's Mysteries of Being Human curriculum will ask you to enter your own darkness, turning your gaze inward, to examine the mystery of how *you* behave, think, and feel. You'll illuminate areas of yourself that have been hanging out on the dark side of the moon, out of sight and, often, out of mind.

Gather your journal and get comfy. Light a few candles to soften your sight. It's time to begin a journey into the mysterious world of you.

SYLLABUS

The idea that knowing yourself as the foundation upon which all other knowledge must be built is not a Night School concept: it dates back to the ancient mystery schools. (That's super-old, Firefly. *The Pyramid Texts,* which date from 3000 BCE, refer to the even older, and now lost, proceedings of the Egyptian mystery schools, which means that the mystery school traditions predate 3000 BCE.) Initiates of these schools—not just the Egyptian, but also Hindu and Chaldean mystery schools—were tasked with knowing themselves first before approaching knowledge of the mysteries.

This tradition carried forward to the place we'll begin our studies: ancient Greece. Travel broadens the mind, Firefly, plus it's reassuring to understand that you aren't alone in your questions but, instead, are part of a long tradition of mystics and seekers who were, like you, just trying to figure themselves out.

From the ancient world, we'll travel forward in time, exploring various theories of the self, circling ever closer to *you.*

You may be wondering: *Why can't we just get to it? Introduce me to me and let's move on!* We all like to learn about ourselves. (That's why silly quizzes designed to tell you which flavor of Jumping Julie's Jellybeans will be your favorite, or which color you should wear during the next lunar eclipse, are wildly, and enduringly, popular.) Unfortunately, the direct approach rarely works with the psyche. You'll want to sidle up slowly as though your own mind were a skittish horse. So while you're welcome to read the last lesson first, you'll find that the winding, gentle, and chronologically linear approach laid out below will yield the best results.

LESSON 1:	Know Thyself
LESSON 2:	The Experimenter Affects the Experiment
LESSON 3:	Step Outside Yourself
LESSON 4:	Maslow's Hierarchy and Why You Need It
LESSON 5:	Caring for Your Self
LESSON 6:	Me and We
LESSON 7:	Nurture vs. Magical Nature
LESSON 8:	Your Personal Path into the Magic
LESSON 9:	The Markers of Blood and Bone
LESSON 10:	The Genealogy of Belonging
LESSON 11:	The Power of Purpose

Remember: one lesson per Night and your homework assignments are due in your journal 72 hours after the lesson is complete.

And don't forget to celebrate the lessons you've finished with the glyph for the moon's phase or a star!

Lesson 1:
KNOW THYSELF

It's story time, Firefly. Light your candles and let's begin.

As promised, we'll begin our tale in ancient Greece, on the steps of the Temple of Apollo in the town of Delphi. Imagine, if you will, the light of the full moon shining on the Doric columns as we climb the marble steps to the portico where we are confronted with this message:

ΓΝΩΘΙ ΣΑΥΤΟΝ

ΜΗΔΕΝ ΑΓΑΝ

ΕΓΓΥΑ, ΠΑΡΑ ΔΑΤΗ

Ε

In case your ancient Greek is rusty, that loosely translates to:

KNOW THYSELF

NOTHING IN EXCESS

SURETY BRINGS RUIN

Eh?

Scholars have been debating that last enigmatic *E* for centuries. Did the stonemason leave for lunch mid-carving and never return? Was he thinking about his sweetheart, Electra, and in his distraction began carving her name?

My personal take is that it's not a letter but, instead, a glyph—an illustration—of how we should interact with the other three precepts. This glyph, which looks like an *E*, represents three lines of thought connected by an upright line, which I understand as a reminder to connect the previous three precepts within the upright being of ourselves.

This idea of being upright—upstanding and moral—was foundational to becoming an initiate at any of the ancient mystery schools, whether you were seeking to matriculate in the Hindu, Chaldean, or Egyptian mysteries. Morality was not something acquired through religious aptitude or an externally derived code of ethics, but was instead a discipline you nurtured within. The mysteries were open only to those who had first mastered themselves, controlling their desires and softening their proclivities.

So here we are, Firefly, standing on the threshold of the Temple of Apollo at Delphi. If the word *Delphi* is tickling the back of your brain, that might be because this particular temple was the home of the famous Oracle at Delphi, also called the *Pythia*, the oracle who pronounced the future of rulers and statesmen . . . and anyone else with coin to pay.

Imagine you're standing at the admission booth to the greatest oracle of the ancient Western world. You've come here because life feels confusing and uncertain and you want someone to tell you clearly what your fate is and what you should do next. But, instead of being reassured that you'll be given an answer to your queries, you're reminded to first know yourself . . . and then to question even that. You weren't admonished to *bow down to the insight of the oracle!* or *prostrate yourself to Apollo!* (Remember, it's his temple, Firefly.) Nope. Instead you were asked to focus inward, to understand yourself, and to not be too self-righteous about it.

Why, you might wonder, is self-knowledge so important that pilgrims were reminded to engage with it before going inside the temple to have their fortune told?

Because prophecies, like much else you will encounter when you put on your Night-goggles, are delivered in allegory and symbol. The meaning is all in the interpretation.

Back at the temple, you pay the admission price, and line up with the other supplicants to ask your question of the Pythia. After months of anticipation, imagine your chagrin when the Pythia extolls:

The golden strawberry is in the mouth of the spring's first snake.

What?! That prophecy is drivel and gobbledygook! You traveled weeks, paid good gold, and got snakes and strawberries . . .

And then, in the middle of your rant, you remember that you were extolled to *Know Thyself.*

So you pause and take inventory. What does a strawberry mean to you? How about a snake?

Knowing yourself—not just on a surface level but at the level of the psyche—is suddenly immensely important. You realize that *you* are the filter through which this prophecy will be interpreted.

Here's another way to think of it, Firefly: if you're stargazing and your telescope has a small smudge just to the right of the center point and, in turn, every star you gaze upon has a small smudge just to the right of the center point, you could spend years developing a theory of why stars disturb the atmosphere on their starboard side. Wouldn't you feel foolish, after years of prognosticating, to realize that the stars aren't smudged, your telescope is?

Standing befuddled outside the Temple of Apollo at Delphi, you realize you are just like that telescope. You need to know where your smudges are and how you refract the light. You need to understand your focal length and your magnification. Everything you study or learn is filtered through the telescope of your perception, which is made up of thoughts, feelings, beliefs, smells, sounds, tastes, prejudices, blind spots, and . . . *stories*. So many stories that you tell yourself about your worth, your lineage, your culture, your smarts. . . . You're made up of stories, stacked one atop the other, creating a psychological city only you can map.

And that is the purpose of this course: to begin to map the stories that make up your personal, magical identity. How you live within these stories influences your perception of the world around you . . . and how the world around you (with its own weight of stories) views you also has a way of pulling perception out of skew.

Picking apart these layers is the only way to make sense of the snakes, strawberries, and other symbols that are the lifeblood of the mystic. The folks who built Apollo's Temple at Delphi knew this and now, hopefully, so do you!

(You may have already noticed that Magical Identity is a more personal class than your other studies at the Night School. Some of your lessons may make your feet itch and your blood run in odd directions. Notice when you're uncomfortable. In those moments, instead of stepping away, pull

out your journal and use it to help unravel the source of your discomfort. Go deeper into the mystery that is you.)

Homework: Begin the Sorting

For tonight's homework, Firefly, you're going to begin working with a process that can help you know a little more about how your heart ticks and your brain tocks.

Here's how to do it:

For the next week, whenever a strong thought, sensation, or emotion crosses your mind, ask yourself: *Really? Why?* Don't overthink this. Trust that the first thing your internal voice says is true even if you don't understand it.

So maybe you think, *I hate ice cream.*

Really? Why? you ask yourself. If you answer, *yes, really, it hurts my stomach* or, *yes, really, the texture is revolting,* then (surprise, surprise) you really do hate ice cream.

But what if you ask yourself *Really? Why?* and you realize that you can't even remember what ice cream tastes like? What you recall instead is that you stopped eating ice cream forever ago, when you were a little kid, because your mom was on one diet after another the entire time you were growing up and she would shoot you these envious looks whenever you ate ice cream in front of her. So you just stopped eating it, because those looks became unbearable. When people asked if you wanted ice cream, you would simply mumble something about not liking it. You said it so many times that it started to feel true . . . But when you get to the root of it, you realize that maybe it's not.

What's your ice cream? What do you think you know about yourself that might not be true? This is your week to find out!

Lesson 2:

THE EXPERIMENTER AFFECTS
THE EXPERIMENT

Physics tells us that the experimenter affects the experiment. In your Night-life, you are the experimenter . . . and sometimes you're the experiment, too. (Where does one start and the other end?)

This precept—that the experimenter affects the experiment—has been proven over and over again, first in the 1970s, when famed theoretical physicist John Archibald Wheeler showed it to be true within the laboratory and, more recently, when a team of scientists led by Francesco Vedovato and Paolo Villoresi of the University of Padua (that's in Italia, Firefly) proved that this same principle holds even when the objects being experimented upon are far away in outer space! Let's first think on the initial lab results: a quantum of light, also called a photon, will behave either like a wave or a particle, depending on how it's measured. This is not like choosing between centimeters and inches, Firefly: we're not talking about two different ways of measuring the exact same thing. We're talking instead about the thing being measured morphing its form to suit the nature of the instrument *doing the measuring*! Imagine that you are going to measure moisture. If you show up with a beaker, the moisture will appear as water, but if you instead have a hygrometer, the moisture will appear as mist. (This is not a perfect analogy, but it gets at just how magical this discovery is!)

So the choice of measuring stick—a decision made by the experimenter—determines whether a photon makes its appearance as a wave or a particle. The intergalactic version of the experiment, which was performed using a laser and satellites, showed that the scientist can make the decision of which measuring stick they will use even after a photon has traveled almost completely back to Earth, magically becoming either the wave or the particle as it arrives in the experimenter's presence.

If this can be true of distant particles of light, imagine the more direct effect you and your decisions will have on all of your mystical workings!

But as you get to know yourself, as you begin to understand the cosmic-dust storms within, you can begin to factor in the effects of how you think, feel, and magically perceive. So, for instance, if you're scrying in a bowl of water and you keep seeing your father, instead of deciding your father's in grave danger and phoning him in a panic, you might pause and think about what your father symbolizes to you. Is he a symbol of joy and hope? Or one of internal conflict and gatekeeping?

Now, in this example *you* are the experimenter. Scrying is the experiment. The precept we discussed earlier tells you that there is no way for you to scry without your thoughts, feelings, and energies becoming involved.

There's one more layer to this moon cake, Firefly, and it's called *sympathetic magic*. This is a less obvious way in which you, the experimenter, might be accidentally slipping your subconscious into the batter. Sympathetic magic has been dubbed, in modern times, *the Law of Attraction*. Whichever name you choose to use, it's an age-old mystical principle that states *like calls to like*. So the very fact of who you are attracts that which is *like* you *to* you. (That sentence is a doozy. Feel free to read it again. And again.) The upshot is, the more you know about *you*, even the bits you don't like to think about, the better you can understand what you are attracting and make shifts, to both your thoughts and your magics, accordingly.

Recognizing the presence of *you* in your magical experiments is foundational to your mystical work. (And in tomorrow Night's lesson, I'll give you the key to begin to get enough distance to see your thoughts and feelings clearly.)

Homework: Measure Your Effect

Let's play with the idea that something as insubstantial as a feeling can change the outcome of an experiment.

To do this, acquire two small versions of the same kind of plant—or you can take two clippings from a plant you already have. Set them up so they are in the same potting medium and getting the same kind of light. Water them both at the same time, giving them identical amounts of water. Everything about the growing conditions for these two plants should be the same.

Now choose one plant that you will shower with positivity. Tell it how beautiful it is and picture the plant growing lush and green. Whenever you walk by it, give it a little love.

Make the other plant your scapegoat. Tell it how horrible it is. Picture it wilted and withering.

Keep this up for a month and see how you, the experimenter, influence the vibrancy of your plants in this experiment! (If this makes you too sad, Firefly, as soon as you notice negative effects, you can reverse course and nurse the object of your negativity back to health with some positive vibes!)

Lesson 3:

STEP OUTSIDE YOURSELF

Tonight we're going to practice stepping outside ourselves—which is neither as difficult nor as easy as you might think!

After last Night's lesson you might be thinking about how very difficult it is to not only know, but control, the thoughts and feelings you are putting out into the world. Tonight's studies will help! You'll learn a tool that will help you get a little distance from your mind's machinations. This will help you to better evaluate your effect on life's mystical experiments.

Let's be clear: This is *not* about your mind stepping away from your body, although you may, subconsciously, think of your mind and body as two separate entities. This cultural confusion is thanks, in large part, to a gentleman named René Descartes. During the 17th century, Descartes postulated that our bodies and minds are made of separate stuff and have different essential natures. As far as he was concerned, the body, made of material stuff, would interact with the physical world while the mind, made of something wispy and immaterial, would operate only within the mental realm. This thinking was the norm for hundreds of years and became an enduring part of the Western cultural mindset.

Perhaps you can see a bit of this dualism in yourself: do you ever say, "my body is X, Y, Z (insert your favorite compliment or insult)"? This linguistic tic of saying "my body," as though it's somehow separate from the rest of you, represents a dualist's way of thinking. If you were not a dualist, you would say "I am X, Y, Z." (You could try it right now, if you like. Gaze up at your favorite constellation and say, *I am made of starstuff.* Doesn't that just feel intergalactic?)

Modern science has shown that the Cartesian way of thinking, as it's called, is bunk (although it did lead to an incredible influx of scientific discoveries, so it could be argued it was a thought exercise worth the centuries given to it). Many of the chemicals that make your mind tick are produced because of your body's reaction to various stimuli. Your mind doesn't exist as an entity separate from your body. Quite the contrary: your mind and body are constantly making and remaking each other.

But your spirit, now that's another story! While your mind is firmly tied to your body, and therefore rather immovable, your spirit has a little more leeway and is perfectly capable of slipping sideways out of your body/mind's protective embrace.

This bit of magic is well known to those who meditate, as well as to method actors, Freudian therapists, and people who journey by spirit. (Some people call those who journey in this way *shamans.* The term *shaman* comes from the Manchu-Tungus word *šaman*, so in some anthropological circles, in order to be a shaman you must be an initiated religious leader from either the Manchu or Tungus tribes, who live in the region of the world that is currently referred to as Russia. But in colloquial culture, the word *shaman* is applied in broader ways. More neutral terms, but with a decidedly New Age glow, are *astral travel* or *astral projection*. Language is tricky and sticky, Firefly. While I'm not sure there's a clear daytime answer to this linguistic linguine, your Night-brain can probably parse "travel by spirit.")

Stepping outside yourself has degrees. You can take a little half step outside of yourself, which is what we're going to learn to do here, or you can take a full step outside of yourself, which puts you in the realm of astral travel or near-death experience. This is a bit much to accomplish without a spotter!

For tonight's homework, instead of learning to leave the room entirely, we are going to practice lingering in a corner, observing our own thoughts but staying decidedly uninvolved and, if possible, judgment-free.

Homework: Step Outside Yourself

We will begin with instructions you may have heard from a meditation teacher, or even a relaxation app: sit quietly and focus on your breath. Allow your thoughts to flow through your mind. Notice them passing by, but try not to focus on them.

Difficult? Absolutely! Our thoughts want our attention, and not paying them any mind can actually make their clamoring louder. A useful trick is to imagine your thoughts are restless children. Affirm what they are signaling and let them know you'll think more about that later.

"Oh, you're right!" you might think. *"A very important point. Let's give that some thought later tonight. Right now we are practicing sitting quietly."*

This bit of active imagining may not feel exactly like meditating . . . but it will quickly get you to your actual objective: stepping outside and observing yourself.

As you practice acknowledging your racing thoughts, you'll start to gain the ability to observe your mental antics without getting entangled in them. Your spirit will notice that your mind is doing its never-ending-thinking thing, but will recognize that all that thinking doesn't have to ruffle your calm.

Shimmying your spirit out of the melees of your mind takes a little practice. It's worth it, though, because from your perch in the corner, you can watch your mind struggle with lessons that might be difficult or trigger-ing. Your spirit can witness your churning feelings as you work through an issue. You can observe yourself and, through observing, begin to see both the body and mind as tools your spirit can use for greater discernment.

Don't you love a good challenge?

MASLOW'S HIERARCHY AND WHY YOU NEED IT

For this evening's lesson, we're going to compare two images side by side. The first image is of something called the chakra system. Remember when I mentioned the ancient Hindu mystery schools? The knowledge of chakras, amongst many other things, is said to have been passed orally between initiates in the northern regions of India. Eventually this oral knowledge was recorded in religious books called the Vedas.

Except you won't find the word *chakra* in these texts: what you'll find instead is the word *cakra* which means "wheel," "disk," and "circular" in San-skrit. It's also a word used to refer to the sun. Cakras are our inner suns: centers of vitality within the physical human body. There were seven *cakras* mentioned in the Vedas, and this is where things get interesting, Firefly: there were seven of a number of other things, including seven rivers that were the lifeblood of the land and seven planets that were thought to form our galaxy.

Whenever you see this type of repetition in an ancient text, you know you've come upon something important hiding in plain view yet offering a glimpse into the mysteries for those who have honed their powers of discernment. This intriguing seven-layer cake of cakras, rivers, planets, and gods delivers a message not spelled out, but implied in the layering: the energy system of the human body mirrors that of the Earth and that of the cosmos, neatly illuminating the principle "as above, so below."

For thousands of years, Hindu mystics worked with the cakras. Like many aspects of religion (all religions, Firefly), their exact use and meaning was likely a subject of discussion among initiates. These discussions would have allowed for evolution over time. When Western spiritualists—during both the Victorian era and the New Age movement—became fascinated by Eastern philosophies, the cakras were used as the basis for the concept of the cakras that non-Hindus are familiar with today.

Through a combination of writings and philosophies from across cultures, our modern conception of the cakras, the one now taught in Western yoga classes and witch covens, was born. In this school of thinking, these centers of vitality control the energy flow in our psychic body, with each cakra having a domain of thought and feeling that it influences. Note here the change that occurred when moving from cakra to chakra: the first was associated with subtle aspects of the physical body, while the second is associated with the psychic body.

(I honestly don't know, Firefly, how those who have a traditional Hindu faith and practice view this shift. On the one hand, religions evolve—you just have to look at the Protestant Reformation to realize this is true—but on the other hand, the modern Western concept of the chakras seems heavily influenced by the Victorian spiritualist movement. Understanding this in greater detail would be a fabulous research project to undertake!) Should we discount the modern interpretation of cakras because it doesn't perfectly match with the original thought? No! Though we should

of course always be mindful of where ideas come from and honor their cultural and cosmic significance, ideas are living: they change and evolve as more information comes to light or as we humans change and evolve. In fact, when things were passed down orally, they were often discussed and not simply digested, as is common with the written word. But just because ideas are meant to grow, change, and evolve like every other living thing, doesn't mean they always grow in the right direction. And even ideas go through the terrible twos and teenage angst. It's always worth examining origins. Indeed, it is necessary for growth and understanding—both the idea's and our own! By tracing where ideas come from, you might notice an intellectual road not taken that you want to explore . . . thus catalyzing another branch in the evolution of thought.

Let's take a closer look at the chakras. Study the image and correspondences below:

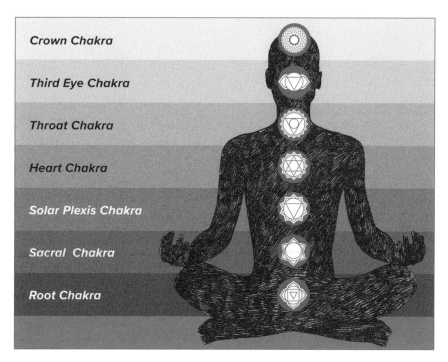

Crown Chakra

Third Eye Chakra

Throat Chakra

Heart Chakra

Solar Plexis Chakra

Sacral Chakra

Root Chakra

Now we're going to compare this modern image of the workings of the chakras, which illustrates our human state seen through spiritual eyes, with a second image, which is our human state seen through the eyes of the science of psychology.

This second image is of Maslow's hierarchy of needs. Abraham Maslow was a research psychologist from 1931 until his death in 1970. Unlike most psychologists of his time who focused on mental illness, Maslow devoted himself to mental wellness, human potential, and self-actualization. He developed a theory that humans must first take care of basic survival needs before they can devote resources to achieving spiritual potential. In a nutshell, saying that before you can wonder about the questions "Why am I here? What is my purpose in this life?" you have to secure the means of actually being here and staying alive.

Maslow's hierarchy of needs looks like this:

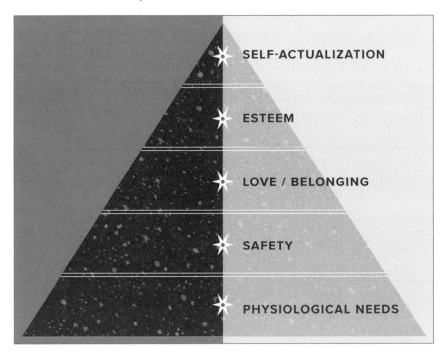

Homework: Scrying the Maps of Self-Actualization

Soften your gaze and contemplate the image of the chakras and the illustration of Maslow's hierarchy of needs. Both are visual representations of how to achieve mystical self-actualization. What do you notice when comparing these two images? Remember, soft gaze, Firefly! Allow your intuition to come out and play.

Try asking yourself these questions:

* **What is similar about these images?**

* **What is different?**

* **What do these images tell you about yourself and where you are in your life's journey? Remember, spiritual journeys seldom run in a straight line! If you look at these images as maps, you may find you've walked in a circle. And that is absolutely okay! All of us circle around, learning what we need to learn, until we are ready to move on.**

* **Is the journey to mystical self-actualization a luxury? Why or why not?**

Be sure to record your thoughts in your journal! You may notice that, like the evolution from *cakra* to *chakra*, your thoughts also evolve over time. Having a written record lets you know where you've been, especially if you need to retrace your thoughts or backtrack to an early incarnation in order to find your way.

Lesson 5:

CARING FOR YOURSELF

You've done some heavy lifting the past few evenings, Firefly. So tonight, let's have a moment of holism because, in addition to being known, your Night-self wants to be nurtured.

"Being nurtured" is going to mean different things to each student at the Night School. For some, it will mean essential oils and a hot foot-bath, while for others a midnight run (safely, of course) is pure bliss. I used to love a run through the city streets after the sun had set. It made me feel both like a visitor and like someone who knew the city intimately and was safe in her shadows. I haven't gone for a midnight run in years. I miss it!

What do you miss, Firefly? Sometimes we forget what nurtures us, or our ideas get skewed by other people's ideas of what's fun, appropriate, or safe.

Think about what self-care truly means to you. What would feel divine right now? (And what's keeping you from doing it?)

Lesson 6:

ME AND WE

Motivational speaker Jim Rohn once posited that each of us is an average of the five people we spend the most time with. Research on social networks conducted by Nicholas Christakis and James Fowler, who looked at 30 years of data, shows that you are influenced by more than simply the five people closest to you: you are also influenced by the people who influence those people! Each of us is like a pebble dropped in a pond, our influence rippling outward in ways the pebble could never imagine as it plummeted through the icy water. You are both an effector and affected by those around you, even the people you don't know.

Perhaps this is why Taoist monasteries were situated on impregnable mountaintops and early Christian mystics became hermits!

Who is influencing your thoughts and attitudes, Firefly? And, more importantly, is their influence supporting your highest self and helping you become the person you want to be? Are you surrounded by those who understand the power of symbols, synchronicities, and signs, or by naysayers who make you doubt yourself and question the inherent magic of the world?

It's time to find out!

Homework: Inventory Your Influencers

From social media to television to the friend who texts every afternoon, we are surrounded by other people's thoughts and feelings. Who's influencing you and what is the nature of their influence? Make a list. Remember, this is not just family and friends; this is also people on social media, the news outlets you turn to for information, the books you choose to read.

After looking at this list, highlight the influencers that support your well-being, happiness, and mystical evolution.

Extra Credit

Now that you have a list of who is affecting your mood and magical mindset, buff and polish your influencer list for greater success! If you have friends who pull you down or are listening to folks who make you feel small, think about shifting your social network.

Remember, this is not about only hanging out with people who agree with you! Take a lesson from the ancient philosophers and have at least one roiling and rollicking debate a week. Seek out people who elevate and challenge you in ways that make you think and feel more deeply. Let them light a fire within you for exploring ideas and diving further into the mysteries of life.

NURTURE VS. MAGICAL NATURE

The modern world is sometimes unfriendly to the magical, mystical side of our beings. Whether through stories learned in a traditional or conservative religious setting, feeling unseen or unheard within your family, or undergoing educational experiences that insisted on a different kind of truth than that which the Night offers up, you may have quashed or quarantined your natural mystic proclivities. These early influences—and the influencers behind them—shaped the way you see the world and how you have felt about exploring life's mysteries. Sifting through them will help you to begin to unknot your own magic.

Tonight, you are the storyteller. Your job this evening is to begin to remember what the magic in your nature looked and felt like before it was changed by the nurture of your upbringing.

This is a tale only you can tell, so pull out your journal and let's get right to (your inner) work!

Homework: The Nature of Nurture

Contemplate the ways in which your early perceptions of the mystic were altered or somehow made "normal." Or, if you are one of the lucky ones who were encouraged to grow into the world of magic and mystery, reflect on how your perceptions have grown and changed and what paths you took to achieve this growth.

Begin by thinking about:

* **what you thought about magic when you were young**

* **how imagination factored into your life**

* **experiences of "seeing" things: ghosts, invisible friends, fairies**

* trancelike experiences

* dreams you remember

* the desire to explore things like astrology or tarot

Now think about how the people in your life responded when you shared these experiences:

* Were you told you were "so cute" or "so creative"?

* Did you hear "you have a magnificent imagination," not as encouragement, but as a line drawn to keep imagination from interfering with the "real world"?

* Were you shushed and told you didn't hear what you thought you heard or didn't see what you thought you saw?

* Were you told your attraction to the mystical tools and channels was evil or against the will of God?

* Were you admonished not to waste your time exploring things like astrology or tarot?

How did these experiences alter how you experienced magic for yourself? What walls did you put up? What wounds never really healed?

Look for the places where you are overly rational or skeptical. Investigate thoughts that feel defensive or ouchy.

If you encounter old angers or fears, use the exercise in lesson 3 (see page 70) to step outside yourself so you can record your observations about your past in your journal without sliding down an emotional rabbit hole. Remember that underneath these hurts, your personal path into the mystery is waiting. Tonight's homework is a step toward uncovering the magic within you. When you are through with this exercise, a good cry for your past self might be in order. Tears are magic: water for flow and salt for protection, pulling out pain, and purifying yourself for what comes next.

Lesson 8:

YOUR PERSONAL PATH
INTO THE MAGIC

Let's start putting some language to the personal, mystical idiosyncrasies you probably began unearthing in last evening's homework, Firefly. A large part of who you are as a seeker of the mysteries will be determined by how you personally perceive the magic of the world around you. Do you see auras or hear voices? Do you commune with ghosts or always know the best moment to ask your boss for a raise?

Each of these skills, and dozens of others, comes from having an awareness of the world around you that extends beyond the five senses you were taught to identify as a child. Everyone has a sixth sense: an ability to take in information beyond the first five senses by reading the energetic patterns around them.

But while everyone has a sixth sense, the ways in which you interpret the energetic information your sixth sense receives are unique to you. Because patterns of energy have no language, your brain translates them into something you find understandable. For some people that means experiencing visions; for others it's hearing voices, understanding patterns, or feeling information in their own body.

There are some words that can help you explore the range of possibilities for interpreting energetic information. I fondly refer to these terms as *The Clairs*.

The Clairs

CLAIRVOYANT: Clairvoyance is associated with your third eye—the eye that sees not the physical world, but the spiritual one. If you see auras or can describe the style of your childhood "imaginary" friend's clothing, then clairvoyance is a tool you use to make sense of the information you're getting from the unseen world.

CLAIRAUDIENT: Did you ever hear voices as a child? Or, when you're thinking of a problem, does a song that seems to answer your issues just happen to play? If so, you are interpreting the energies of the world with clairaudience, your brain translating the invisible patterns of the world into sound.

CLAIRCOGNIZANT: Do you recognize patterns easily? Or perhaps sometimes you know the answer to a problem without knowing how you know? Maybe when you're doing web searches, you know which of the zillions of entries that a search engine pulls up are worth opening and reading further. This is claircognizance: clear knowing.

CLAIRSENTIENT: Those who are clairsentient know in their bodies. If your palms always itch when someone lies to you, or if you read about an herb and feel the illness it treats in your body, then you are displaying clairsentience. This can be a difficult Clair to recognize! If you suspect you're clairsentient, keep a journal. Note strong physical sensations and what is happening in the world around you at the time that you feel them. This can help you figure out how your physical sensations are conveying information.

CLAIRALIENCE & CLAIRGUSTANCE: these less common Clairs are particularly sensual! Clairalience is when your brain translates the energy patterns you perceive as scent, while clairgustance reveals energies as taste. If you're meditating and suddenly smell your grandpa's cigar or if you know a thunderstorm is coming because you taste saltwater taffy, you're familiar with these seriously sensual Clairs.

By the light of day, the Clairs might feel like fairy godmothers: the wispy dream of a mystical imagination. But by the shine of the stars, when objects and ideas soften around the edges, they will come and kiss you on the cheek, reminding you of a depth of knowing you may have forgotten you have.

Still, it's easy for the mind to feel doubtful. If yours does, feed it this factoid:

With synesthesia, a condition recognized by modern medicine and science, one perceptual or cognitive pathway automatically triggers a second. So, for a synesthete, sound might be translated into color, taste, or scent . . . And next to this bit of magic, the Clairs seem positively mundane!

Homework: Inventory Your Innate Magics

Let's uncover more about your mystical potential!

Often our own earliest proclivities show us exactly how we relate to the spiritual side of life. This evening, you're going to take inventory of your earliest memories of things that felt magical. Did you see fairies? Hear voices? Have an invisible friend or talk to the family cat? Did you know who was coming to visit before they showed up?

Let's take a walk down memory lane. Have your journal handy in case you need it.

Begin by closing your eyes and breathing steadily in and out. Don't force it or try fancy yogic breathing tricks! Simply inhale and exhale.

Now count backward from your current age to the age of seven. Each breath represents one year as you wind back time and revisit your past self. When you get to seven, sit with your seven-year-old self and remember. How did you see the world? How did you let the magic in?

If seven is a magic number for you, then record what you've learned in your journal. But if you still need more information, or if you had already tamed your inner magic by the age of seven, go back to six or five or even to four.

After you have recorded what you have learned, count yourself back up to your present year.

This last bit is important, Firefly. Get into the habit of returning to your starting point so that your spirit fully returns to your body whenever you put yourself in a light trance like this. Mystics know the messiness of inadvertently leaving doors open to the past and the deeper subconscious realms. Set yourself a goal: make shutting mystical doors behind you as second nature as making your bed in the morning—because otherwise, as with your bed, it's tempting to tumble back through those open psychic portals.

Lesson 9:

THE MARKERS OF BLOOD AND BONE

Sometimes I imagine the Clairs live in an as-yet-unsequenced genome within each of our double helices or that they are among the hidden gems in the pile of extras called junk DNA. On the one hand, this seems fanciful, but on the other, the highly individual markers of blood and bone have long been a part of the magical compendium—we just lacked a name for the material being worked with until recently.

While DNA is a relatively new scientific discovery (first identified in the late 1860s by Swiss chemist Friedrich Miescher), the idea that each human has a unique signature, which is contained and replicated in every part of our bodies, is ancient. This is the principle "as above, so below" at play once again: each piece of our body contains the genetic information of the whole: saliva, hair, fingernail clippings, and blood are microcosms of the macrocosm of you. As such, these elements have been used in magic to act as an energetic arrow, directing a spell toward a specific individual. Poppets, or dolls made to symbolize a person, are usually activated with a bit of hair. Sacred promises—blood oaths—have been marked with the red stuff from time immemorial.

Although the ancients didn't know what DNA was, its distinctive double helix has been symbolically present since the 21st century BCE, when it appeared in a vase dedicated to the Sumerian god Ningishzida. *Ningishzida* loosely translates from Sumerian as "Lord of the Giving Tree." (Allow your thoughts to be fluid, Firefly: *Lord of the Giving Tree . . . Tree of Life . . . Family Tree . . . hmm.*) The looping spirals of our genetic code are again seen on the caduceus of the Greek god Hermes, who began his godhood as a deity of the underworld and was later promoted to chief messenger for the gods. This put him in a unique position to observe the spirals of life and death. It's not only within the Mesopotamian region that the double helix makes itself known: it is woven into the designs of the Aztec, Maori, and Celts at a time when there was little intercontinental travel to explain its far-flung influence. Graphically, these intertwined helices are sometimes depicted as snakes, which aligns them with representations of kundalini energy flow in the human body, as well as with the oldest stories of the Jewish and Christian Bible, in which the snake delivers knowledge of good and evil. So while we generally think of DNA as a scientific phenomenon, it also has a rich symbolic presence: its energetic fingerprint has appeared across the globe since our earliest recordings of history.

What does DNA mean for your mystical life? What is the place of blood and of blood ancestors in your magical work?

There is no one answer to this question, my Little Genome, but exploring it will give you insight into who you are and who you want to become. There's a good chance that you've given your blood, your DNA, and your lineage a tremendous amount of thought already. What I want you to do now is put on your Night-goggles and revisit the texture of your thoughts and feelings when viewing blood through the lens of mysticism. The ways in which we understand DNA in our daylight lives—for instance looking at your double helices for genetic diseases—may not be the same as the musings that emerge when you view the same information through your

Night lenses. And that's okay. You can hold multiple truths at the same time. The mystic often sees what *should be*, instead of what is.

As you think about the place of blood, of DNA, of ancestry, bear in mind that we are approaching this question from a very particular point in history. Our ability to clearly define who we are genetically is unique, and it's worth remembering that this clarity of knowing was not a luxury our ancestors had. In the past, households were multigenerational and might include spouses as well as orphans or apprentices. There was no blood test to determine our origins and ancestry, so people remembered who they were through stories passed down from one generation to the next—and we all know how muzzy those tales can become! It was not unusual for favorite students to be adopted into a lineage and thought of as the child of their teacher.

It's important to begin to contemplate how you feel about this because mystical work can involve calling on your ancestral line. How do you want to define *ancestors* and what is the role of blood going to be (if any) in your personal definition?

An additional thing to consider as you ponder the mysteries of blood and bone:

Have you ever visited a historic house? Like Betsy Ross's homestead in Philadelphia or Red House in London? These homes, now museums, were originally built to be lived in. For decades they housed the daily comings and goings of regular people. But at some point, often due to the burden of taxes on future generations, they were given to the state. This is the point at which curators came in and had to make a decision: what is the most significant date in this house's history? Once decided, they restored the home to that date, destroying what came after and disregarding what came before.

When you look at your DNA profile and declare yourself Ethiopian or German, Celtic or Chinese, realize that you're stopping your DNA clock at a carefully curated moment in time. Ethiopia began to appear as a separate state as early as the second century CE, and mention of the German region can be traced back to Julius Caesar, who ruled Rome in 46–44 BCE. The bloodlines in your DNA are more ancient than this. The Celtic and Chinese cultures are older still, evolving from around 1200 BCE and 1600 BCE respectively . . . yet your bloodline predates both of these venerable civilizations. Your bloodline, and the bloodline of every other human on this planet, goes back to the first women, who are sometimes referred to as Mitochondrial (mt) Eve. They were thought to have lived about 200,000 years ago in Southern Africa. What does it feel like to think about these women being the ancestors of us all?

Allow yourself to dream on all this over many moons, so you can begin to sense how your Night-self relates to blood and belonging. (And remember, Firefly, the Night-mind can hold multiple truths at the same time. Your thoughts don't have to follow the rationality of daytime!)

Homework: The Role of DNA

Contemplate the role you want DNA to have in your personal spiritual practices. How closely will DNA be tied to your individual search for a path to the mystery and magic of life? How do you feel about learning from, and in turn, sharing with, those who are from cultures that are outside your most recent blood-bound heritage? Do you feel it's necessary to create rules for yourself or others around the cross-cultural sharing of mystical experiences? Why or why not?

Lesson 10:

THE GENEALOGY OF BELONGING

To the modern mind, the idea of a student or apprentice being adopted into a family sounds alternately romantic and absurd. In the West, in particular, we're used to not only an unassailable nuclear family unit, but also a systematized adoption process. Adoption is not something that can simply be agreed upon between the involved parties in our current culture: there are interviews, and wait times, and legal documents, oh my! Additionally, we don't expect to have one teacher we learn from over many years, but instead a multiplicity of teachers and information from numerous sources at our fingertips. The idea of being deeply connected through a lineage of learning—and perhaps so deeply entrenched in it that you become the family of the teacher—is something we've forgotten how to feel.

But lineage is not just genetics and family connections: it's the acknowledgment of the energies that support you and help you to grow. Who and what has supported you as you have grown into yourself?

Acknowledging lineage creates a profound sense of trust and belonging, it reminds you that you are not the first person to walk your particular path. When you remember that you are part of a lineage, you realize that you are a conduit: that knowledge is passing through you on its way to someone else. (So no hoarding, Firefly!)

If you are at odds with your family of origin, or out-of-sync with the religious codes you grew up with, acknowledging a lineage of learning can help you feel a part of something that stretches back through the ages. Lineage anchors you to ancestral energy: the power of those who came before, whether they share your DNA or your passion for botany or your love of the stars.

As wisdom gets democratized and shared by a myriad of voices, we can sometimes lose our sense of lineage. When we read information online, we don't feel linked to the chain of learning. We lack a sense of support, of groundedness, on our path. We lose the awe and honor of being a trusted keeper of hard-won knowledge passed from generation to generation.

Homework: Create Your Mystical Family Tree

Anchor your spiritual identity by drawing the family tree of your mystical lineage.

Include those who are blood relations (if you so choose), as well as those in your intellectual lineage, a lineage of craft, or a lineage of affiliation, as a way of anchoring your spiritual identity.

If you need a beginning point, start a list of who (and what!) you've learned from over the years, noting both your favorite and also your difficult teachers. And be sure to note, Firefly, those teachers who would not be recognized by the light of day: ghosts, familiars, invisible friends, the rabbit who hung out near you when you were a child or the wind that whispered its secrets. This exercise is for you and you alone, so be honest with yourself and, through your honesty, honor those—human or not—who have shared wisdom with you.

Lesson 11:

THE POWER OF PURPOSE

As we wrap up our studies of the Mysteries of Being Human, Firefly, I want to pose some final questions:

What's your *why*?

and

What will you do with the magic you discover at the Night School?

Are you using your studies for escape? To salve your ego? To soothe your curiosity?

Why are you interested in unraveling the mysteries of being human? Why is the mystic appealing to you?

Will you begin to heal yourself? Guide others to heal?

Create something new in the world? Explore the places where sciences and magic meet?

Begin a sacred practice? Create sacred spaces for others?

Support the growing things of the earth? Work with the powers of decay (the first step to regeneration)?

Commune with non-embodied beings? Stand at the crossroads and help others through life's changes?

Be honest with yourself about what you are seeking. Your desires are part of who you are and there are so many ways to bring your Night studies into the daylight world!

This is your invitation to begin noodling on this topic. You don't have to hound down your purpose. It's already embedded within you. Offer a gentle invitation for it to come out and play over the coming weeks!

Homework: Be with the Questions

It's okay not to know all the answers today. Be with these questions. Imagine they are seeds you have planted to help yourself grow.

Extra Credit

Ready to dive deeper into the Pandora's box this course may have opened in the deep recesses of your mind? Choose a book from the Additional Semester Readings list and keep going!

ADDITIONAL READINGS AND RESOURCES

The search for self is a story we humans return to over and over again. It's very hard not to overwhelm you, Firefly, with a list of every novel I've ever devoured end to end. While reading novels may seem to be an exercise in delving deeply into the lives of fictional characters, perhaps that urge may point instead to a search for mirrors—even fictional—of one's own thoughts and feelings. Through books we find validation and intimacy with ourselves. Additionally, the words become a doorway, another way to step into the collective unconscious.

You can find this experience in whatever novels are whispering to you. As you read, notice how the characters are searching to know themselves, express themselves, face their own demons and fears. How are they learning about themselves? What are they learning about themselves? And, perhaps most importantly for our purposes here, how does this mirror your own journey?

If you want an additional road map for your inner work, Martha Beck is a guide who knows the Night. Try *Steering by Starlight* or *Finding Your Own North Star*. Another rocket ship into the inner sanctum of your heart is Oriah Mountain Dreamer's *The Invitation*.

If you're wanting to learn more about how the bits of you—body, mind, emotion, and spirit—work together, these books will help you with the science:

* *Descartes' Error*, Antonio Damasio

* *The Biology of Belief*, Bruce Lipton

* *Molecules of Emotion*, Candace Pert

If you desire additional ways to step outside yourself, meditation will offer a myriad of approaches. For a how-to book, try *A Woman's Book of Meditation* by Hari Kaur Khalsa. For a less straightforward approach, Lama Surya Das's *Make Me One with Everything* might suit.

While I'm not in a position to instruct on it, exploring racial trauma is an important thread in the healing of our modern societies. One of the wisest voices I've heard on this broad topic is Resmaa Menakem. The read: *My Grandmother's Hands: Racialized Trauma and the Pathway to Mending Our Hearts and Bodies.*

Want to explore gender and/or sexual identity? Both of the books below include essays, so you get a variety of voices on the topic (because if there's anything I'm sure of, Firefly, both these topics are not one size fits all):

* *The ABCs of LGBT+* by Ashley Mardell

* *Every Body* by Julia Rothman and Shaina Feinberg

Extra, Extra Credit

As I mentioned, the Pythia (aka the Oracle of Delphi) is both a mentoress and a cautionary tale for those of us who study the Night. *Why?* you might wonder. Do a little research and see if you can figure it out. Start by consulting Grandma Google to learn what is known of the Pythia. Think about these things:

* **Who interpreted the Pythia's prophecies?**

* **What outside influences were woven into her pronouncements?**

* **Were the Pythias—and there were many, many priestesses who performed these duties over the centuries, not just one—doing anything that might be dangerous to their own psyches?**

divining the night

(Divination 101)

DIVINING THE NIGHT IS AMONGST OUR MOST POPULAR courses at the Night School. You're lucky to be registered, Firefly. We have to run a lottery every year because everybody wants in.

Despite the course's popularity, students sometimes feel disappointed that learning the art of divination won't allow them to infallibly make millions in the stock markets or 100 percent accurately predict which job offer will create a joyous future.

There is nothing "infallible" or 100 percent accurate about divining, Firefly. Divination is about seeking patterns. It's a soft and squishy way of navigating the swirling geographies of time and space.

Wait! you might be thinking, *"knowing" shouldn't be soft and squishy.* That's why here at the Night School we identify two ways of knowing.

The first is the knowing of your daylight mind, a form of knowing that wants to be rational and absolute—the day-brain often refuses to remember that it can be faulty, manipulated, or just plain wrong! *Truths*, says the day-brain, *should be clear and precise so that they can stand up to the scrutiny of the noonday sun.*

Then there's Night-knowing, which specializes in the truths of the heart, soul, or body, none of which are tied to the rationality of the day. Dreams, journeys of the imagination, intuitions, and our spiritual beliefs fall into this second category. These ways of knowing are suited to the interstitial times of dusk and dawn, as well as the inky darkness of the Night, when edges soften and the heart's truths don't sound at all absurd. Your Nighttime self knows that life is comprised of multilayered shadows and things half seen . . . and it revels in these mysteries!

(If you want to go down the rabbit hole of *how* we know, Firefly, one place to start is with Aristotle's *Nicomachean Ethics*. In it, Aristotle identifies three ways of knowing. But don't breathe a sigh of relief and think that's the final answer. Almost two millennia later, John Locke, an English physician and philosopher, also identified three types of knowledge. Wouldn't it have been brilliant if Locke confirmed Aristotle's observations? But, no such luck. Locke's three ways of knowing are completely different from Aristotle's! All this to say, the professional thinkers of the world are constantly rearranging the puzzle pieces, trying to figure out how our human minds work. That's why we keep it simple, Firefly: day-brain and Night-brain.)

It's important to remember that neither form of knowing is "right" and both are not only valid, but necessary. To live wholly, we must find balance, the same way we balance light and dark and inhale and exhale. (Refresh your sense of balance by rereading Foundations lesson 8 on page 48.) The daylight mind thrives on what is conscious, but the Night-mind seeks the hidden.

And so divination is a ramble round the twisting paths of time, a pit stop at the crossroads of cosmos, a tea date with the Pythia. It's flying Magic 8-Balls and incoherent mutterings that have been reinterpreted, over and over again, for millennia. Divination is a waking dream . . . and a dreaming wake. In other words, divination is 100 percent pure Night. It's untamable, unpredictable, soft and squishy 'round the edges, and utterly delicious!

So dust off your crystal ball and get cozy in your moon-phase pj's: let's waltz through the steps of divination and then cha-cha into a few safety protocols before you're off to the divination laboratory.

SYLLABUS

Divination has been around forever, and during those eons, people have used everything from bones to entrails to the flight patterns of birds to predict the future. Here at the Night School, we believe this journey can take you into the past, present, or future. (Time is a whole other topic, but suffice to say the idea that it's linear is so 19th century: Einstein irrevocably upended the linear timeline theory.)

Divination is a multistep process, which starts with getting clear on your question and ends with interpreting the answer you receive. Divination requires the combined, and perhaps seemingly contradictory, skills of close observation and fluid imagining, making it much more art than science.

Note that Divining the Night is a theory course. Together we'll walk through the process of divining (without actually performing a divination). We save the practical experience for the Divination Lab—Tools of the Mystic—which will be your first course in the next semester.

This course is a step-by-step recipe for cooking up delicious divinations:

LESSON 1:	Observe the Patterns
LESSON 2:	Craft the Right Question
LESSON 3:	Choose the Type of Divination
LESSON 4:	Create a Tabula Rasa
LESSON 5:	Do the Divination
LESSON 6:	Record the Results
LESSON 7:	Interpret Your Divination
LESSON 8:	Don Your Safety Goggles!

A final reminder before you dive in:

* One lesson per Night.

* Your homework assignments are due in your journal 72 hours after the lesson is complete.

* Marking off the lessons as you finish feels like a high five and a sip of champagne all rolled into one.

* And don't skip ahead to the lab before you do the theory, Firefly. I see you side-eyeing the pages between here and there!

(I know your palms are itching to pull out your oracle cards *right now,* but with a little patience, the lessons in Divining the Night will set you up for success. Just like in high school chemistry lab, you need to understand the ingredients and tools you're working with before you begin mixing them willy-nilly. And just like in chemistry lab, things can go *BOOM!* if you're unaware of what you're doing and leave the ethyl alcohol too close to the Bunsen burner.)

OBSERVE THE PATTERNS

Let's begin with the much underrated skill of spotting synchronicities and noticing patterns in the world around you. Your ability to divine accurately relies on an aptitude that may seem sideways to oracle-izing: that of *observing*.

Observing lets you begin to feel into the warp and weft of reality. Witnessing the cycle of the stars and listening to the susurrus of the ocean's waves remind us that we're part of something greater, something with its own patterns. When we perform divination, we're traveling ancient pathways, woven both into the Earth's beginnings as well as our own psyches. Patterns, which contain the accreted wisdom of the human soul, are one doorway into the place Carl Jung referred to as the collective unconscious, where symbols and stories linger, waiting for you to blunder along and tap into their secrets.

To begin to cultivate this way of being, practice walking through your life with open eyes, senses, and awareness, just like you did in your Orientation exercise. There are patterns swirling all around you, and recognizing one when you see it is a skill necessary for divining. Practice this heightened awareness not only during the Night but also throughout the day. Make it your new normal to pay attention to the sighs of the wind, the flight paths of the birds, and the whispers of the leaves . . . they all have a story to tell if you're willing to listen. Live in the city? Not a problem! You still have birds and trees and stars. You also have the patterns of people, which can be just as fascinating. Observe how they stand on subway platforms or in line to get coffee. (Try to be subtle about it, Firefly: gaping will introduce you to a different kind of bird.) Once you start truly seeing, you'll realize there are patterns everywhere.

After a few weeks of increased noticing, expand your vision: look for shifts and changes to the usual patterns you've come to expect. These unusual observations are a sign that something new and different is occurring. If, for example, you see three wild turkeys over the course of a week and you usually see none, pay closer attention. What are the wild turkeys doing? Where do you see them? Do a little research: Do wild turkeys migrate? Are you on a migratory route? Open yourself up to changes that might be happening in the physical world or in the unseen realms of spirit.

Pay attention to the things that are drawing your attention. That seems obvious, doesn't it? But in our busy lives we often make and discard observations faster than a dog sheds hair. Try to slow yourself down and actually notice what you're noticing. Observe the usual patterns and the unusual occurrences, notice things that may be signs or symbols, contemplate how you feel or what you think when you see a certain image, and then try to step outside your thoughts and feelings and back into a place of observation.

Our brains desperately seek meaning. Learning to switch this meaning-making proclivity on and off is a skill that will come in handy as you immerse yourself in the ways of the oracles. Instead of trying *not* to have a thought or feeling about what you're noticing, catalog your affinities, and your aversions. Learning to both understand your own biases and notice the world around you without jumping into meaning-making will be one of your most important tools in connecting with deeper knowing and mapping future possibilities.

Homework: Sketch Your Surroundings

Sketching can get your brain to shift gears from judging and meaning-making into simply noticing.

For this evening's exercise, Firefly, attempt to draw either the room you're sitting in or an object within that space. For instance, you could doodle out the dimensions of your comfy armchair, adding in the antique piecrust table you inherited from your grandmother. You could sketch the philodendron in the corner and the framed photo which, you will suddenly notice, is hanging slightly askew above it. Try to capture the exact drape and fold of your lap blanket (which will be difficult unless you're an expert drawer but try anyway because it will make you focus in on details).

Or instead you could go small and try to depict only the juncture of where the leaf of the philodendron merges with the stem. You might think you're taking the easy option but, as you study the joint, you'll notice a surprising number of shades of green—lime and forest, celadon and jade. If you continue to look carefully, you'll realize there's a dry brown sheath on the leaf that has a swirling fold with an almost white edge.

It's this act of close observation, which occurs when you put pen or pencil to paper, that matters, not the final drawing. (You can throw your sketch away as soon as you're done.) Pay attention to details and edges and how objects relate to each other. Notice the shadows thrown by your lamps and candles, the patterns of the fur on the face of your cat, and the way the spines of your books align.

Ferreting out this level of detail will help you decipher the nuances of your visions, dreams, and divinations.

Lesson 2:
CRAFT THE RIGHT QUESTION

Every divination starts with a question, Firefly . . . except when it doesn't.

I can't tell you how often I see students grab an oracle deck, pull a card, read the meaning from the wee guidebook, and apply that meaning to whatever situation first comes to their mind.

> Ooo! This card says "you're beginning a new cycle." That's so exciting! I bet I'm going to get a promotion.
>
> or
>
> Oh no. This card is all about death. My grandmother! I'm so worried!

But these cards were pulled with no particular question in mind. What if you were a person with a womb feeling an ache in your lower back and the twinge in your middle when you pulled the first card? Does tracking those physical sensations change how you'd interpret a card that has to do with "beginning a cycle"?

The question begins the divination process. If there is no particular question, then the information you get could be about anything: the last thought you had, the state of your body, your current circumstance . . . The possibilities are endless!

A divination exists in relation to a query. Without a question, you're just listening to the white noise between radio stations. So the first step is coming up with a question. But not all questions are created equal!

Compare these two queries:

* **What should I do next?**

* **Should I take the new position I was offered today?**

Now compare these two:

* **Should I take the new position I was offered today?**

* **Will I be happy in the new position I was offered today?**

The quality of the question determines the quality of the answer. Do you want to know what's best for your bank account? For your emotions? For your relationship with your partner?

The more specific you can be, the more pertinent information you can get and the less chance you'll think your divination is about your grandmother dying when it's actually about your car making a trip to the metal junkyard in the sky.

Once you have a clear and concise question, write it at the top of a fresh journal page before you begin the divining process.

Homework: Get Good at Asking Questions

Tonight you're going to hone your question-asking skills, Firefly. Here's how:

* Write down the first question that comes to your mind. Don't over-think it.

* Now edit that question to make it more specific.

* Finally, look at your edit and ask yourself if it's detailed enough. Think about what you really want to know.

If you aren't sure what the "best" solution might mean in a particular situation, try working with the words "for my highest good and the highest good for all involved." This leaves room for the magic of the world to bring you unexpected treasures.

Rewrite the question one last time, getting as granular as possible on the details you want to explore.

Your work might look like this:

* Should I get a puppy?

* Should I get the puppy I cuddled at the pound this morning?

* Will the puppy I cuddled at the pound this morning grow into a dog that will suit my family's lifestyle?
      or

* Will bringing home the puppy I cuddled at the pound this morning be for my highest good and the highest good for all involved?
      or

* Is this puppy part of the pattern of my future?

Remember, your highest good might involve replacing the sofa cushion the puppy pees on. "Highest good" doesn't mean "without aggravation." Sometimes we learn from life's annoyances, and often there's something beautiful waiting to happen that transcends the obstacles we encounter on the journey to get there.

Now it's your turn! Work on asking not just a good question but the question that elicits the type of answer that will help you make your decisions.

Lesson 3:

CHOOSE THE TYPE OF DIVINATION

We're at step 3, Firefly: *Choose the best type of divination to answer your question.* Let's figure out which of the prophetic pickings is just right for you.

Obviously, in order to do that, you need to know what your options are. There are many!

Imagine an old wooden chest with a curved rosewood top. The lock is no longer shiny, and the hinges open slightly sideways from centuries of the lid being lifted. Inside is a jumble of treasures and odd objects that make you wonder if maybe someone was storing stage props. Whoever packed this trunk was most definitely not a neatnik. Everything is just tossed in willy-nilly!

That, Firefly, is a pretty accurate description of the Trunk of Divination. For just about forever all sorts of things have been tossed in—mirrors and gazing balls, crystals and cards. It's all glittery, alluring, and potentially magical, but there is little rhyme or reason.

This is the trunk we're going to unpack, sorting it into piles for ease of understanding. There will definitely be some objects left out, but we should be able to create a smidge of order. The Trunk of Divination holds a few millennia's worth of stuff. We'll explore some, but not all, of it in the labs in the second part of class.

Grab a breath of moonshine, settle into your favorite armchair, and let the sorting begin!

We're going to sort the tools of divination into four categories. Note that the tools in each category can be used in a variety of ways—and each one is presented in the Tools of the Mystic (your next course). But for now we're focused on how these tools are used for gazing into the murky depths of time, so the categories created will reflect that. The four categories are:

* tools for amplifying your intuition

* tools for scrying the collective unconscious

* tools for reading the micro patterns

* tools for reading the macro patterns

Tools to Amplify Your Intuition

Your body is a finely tuned receiver. It's constantly reading information from the world around you. But most of this information comes in forms your conscious brain can't quite process unless you've worked to develop your Clairs (see page 83). So all this incoming data is registered by your day-brain as not particularly useful, and it gets stored in your subconscious.

Tools that amplify your intuition help you to pull this information forward and give it a form your conscious mind can work with. The tools below draw the intuitive information you're already receiving—for instance the input you get from your personal Clair—into the visible spectrum. By making the invisible visible, they help you understand the messages you're receiving from the world around you.

The main tools in this category are:

* pendulums

* smoke

* freewriting

* dreaming

* pattern work (for some, this can activate intuition)

Scrying the Collective Unconscious

You'll have a full lesson on the collective unconscious in just a bit. For now, know that the forms of divination that create an entry point into the collective unconscious include:

* oracle cards and individual tarot card pulls (full spreads fall into the "reading the macro patterns" category, Firefly)

* bibliomancy

* active imagining

* some forms of scrying

Reading the Micro Patterns

There's a pattern to the universe. The principle *as above, so below* reminds us that the pattern is discernible in every aspect of creation, small and large (see lesson 10 of Midnight Foundations on page 51). In the plant world, this has been called the Doctrine of Signatures. Each plant is said to show us what its medicine is by the shape of its leaves, the colors of its flowers, and the particulars of its growth habits.

You can approach the entirety of the pattern by looking at a small piece of it—reading the micro—which is like looking at one tree and, from careful observation of its health and growth habits, using it to get an idea of what's going on in the entire forest.

Ways of doing this include:

* reading tea leaves, oil splotches, bones, stones, etc. (in all of these forms of divination, the pattern you're seeing is a microcosm of the forces at work in the life of the person querying)

* some forms of scrying

* palm and facial reading (we won't cover this in the labs because it takes specific knowledge. Check the Library for books that will point you in the right direction!)

Reading the Macro Patterns

You can also approach the pattern from the other direction: by reading the macro. When you read the macro, you go big. You look at the entirety of the forest and, by knowing where the water is, the state of the soil, and how much sun and air circulation the trees are getting, discern the patterns and what they can tell you about the individual trees within that landscape.

Tools for reading the macro include astrology and tarot. These systems are necessarily vast because they're divining by looking at large patterns of past, present, and future. Some of the building blocks for tarot are woven into your Elemental Alchemization course (see page 153) and Harnessing the Celestial Tides gives you a groundwork for astrology (see page 193). But both will also require extensive self-study. Check the Extra Credit section for recommended readings.

Homework: Gather Your Supplies

If you haven't already, begin to gather your supplies for Semester 2. The list is on page 126.

Lesson 4:

CREATE A TABULA RASA

You're getting very close to the moment of casting your divination, Firefly! Remember that, in your Divination Labs, you'll want to run through the pre-steps we're going over here before you do your divination experiment.

We're at the final step before the big moment. Once you have your question ready and you've chosen your type of divination, you'll want to clear your mind and energy field so that you can see clearly. I think of this as creating a *tabula rasa*.

A tabula rasa was the ancient Roman equivalent of a blank notepad. Instead of being made of paper, it was made with wax. The wax was "blanked" by heating it and then smoothing it out. The same tablet could then be used over and over. A tabula rasa is like a new moon evening when the stars are obscured: an inky void, full of nothing but possibility.

Let's gently warm your mind and smooth over the constellations of past impressions so you can bring your divination to a clean Night sky. This is much like removing the smudges from the telescope lens. (Remember that metaphor from the Mysteries of Being Human?) By creating a tabula rasa, you're preparing yourself both mentally and energetically to receive clearly.

There are many ways to "blank" yourself, and over time you'll develop your own rituals for grounding, centering, and getting clear. Tonight, I'm going to suggest four ways. After you read them and check for necessary ingredients in your pantry or magical supplies cupboard, choose one to do for homework.

Breathe and Visualize

This is your do-anywhere method for getting yourself clean, clear, and ready to work.

Get comfortable, making sure your spine is relatively straight so the air can move in and out of your lungs easily. Breathe slowly into your belly, imagining the air moving down your spine. Gently release your breath.

On your next breath, picture breathing in the stillness of a new moon Night. Inhale the velvet darkness, letting it soothe your troubles and worries. Breathe out jumbles of words, stray thoughts, and sticky feelings—both your own and anyone else's you may be carrying around.

Keep going, pulling clarity and quiet in through your lungs, exhaling everything that doesn't belong to you and your energy body, until all that remains is a tabula rasa ready to receive a divination.

Salt and Soak

Salt is used for its ability to pull out water from other substances by drawing moisture to the surface. You'll find it used in traditional embalming methods and in the kitchen to "salt out" meats and veggies.

On a chemical level, salt reduces the solubility of certain molecules, so it is also traditionally used for protection. Finally, if you "salt the earth," nothing can grow there, so metaphorically, salt keeps other people's thoughts and feelings from growing on you.

What does this have to do with creating a tabula rasa? Water is used to symbolize emotions. Use a salt bath to draw your emotions to the surface so you can release them and "salt out" energies that aren't yours. After you send the muck down the drain, you'll notice that the salt has left a lovely protective layer against your skin.

Fill the tub, add a cup of either sea salt or mineral salt, light some candles, and let the combination of the salt and heat do the work of drawing up and releasing as you relax.

Let It Go to Smoke

Have you ever seen an image of a priest walking down the aisle of a cathedral, swinging a holey metal baseball on a long chain? That ball and chain is called a censer. Inside of it is incense.

Incense is simply dried herbs and resins, which are burned. In fact, burning is the key attribute of incense: the word comes from the Latin *incendere*, which means "to burn." This practice stretches across time and around the globe. Ancient Egyptians offered each other bouquets of dried combustible herbs, Babylonians burned incense while waiting for divination, and incense burners have been found in many parts of Asia. The word *perfume* actually comes from the French *per fume*, which means "by the smoke." It refers to women's practice of throwing herbs on the fire and then drying their hair by the scented flames.

Modern incense comes in many forms: resins and powdered herbs made into cones or sticks, loose dried herbs which are burned on a charcoal disk (or, if you have a fire going, simply thrown on the flames), or a clump of dried herbs which might be tied with a string—these are now usually called "bundles" instead of "incense." The smoke from burning the plant material wafts through your aura, allowing the cleansing properties of the herbs to get into your metaphysical nooks and crannies while the scent soothes your nerves and quiets your mind.

Shake, Rattle, and Roll

Vibration will dislodge even the most stubborn metaphysical muck! If dancing it out is your preferred method of relieving stress, grab a rattle and give your aura a rinse at the same time.

No rattle? No problem. Dried beans, or rice, or paper clips in a mason jar will do the trick just fine. Rattle all around yourself as you move your body. If an area of your aura feels like it needs an extra shake or two, trust the sensation. You can add a visualization by imagining anything stuck to you vibrating right off, as any bits of you that have become calcified soften and melt like wax. You'll have a fresh tabula rasa in no time!

Homework: Test-Drive a Tabula Rasa Ritual

Choose from one of the above methods of creating your tabula rasa and take it for a test drive!

Extra Credit: Find Your Shorthand

As delightful as a candlelit soak can be, taking a bath every time you want to use your pendulum is going to get old really fast. Coming up with a shorthand for your long-form ritual will be immensely helpful. So, for instance, if a salt bath works for you, imagine other ways of using salt and water to achieve the same end. Could you wash your hands with a salt scrub, imagining everything you're releasing flowing down the drain? Or dip your hands in salt water and give your aura a cat bath with your salty-wet hands?

(I personally love salt, Firefly. Those little salt packets at take-out restaurants make it easy to do a quick cleanse when I'm away from home.)

Come up with your own mini-version for your larger Tabula Rasa ritual. Can you clear yourself with one breath? Shake your car keys as a rattle? Absolutely. It's a matter of training your energy field to respond quickly to whatever trigger you create.

Try a few things and see what feels best for you. Put your day-brain to bed and let your Night-mind play!

Lesson 5:

DO THE DIVINATION

When you get to your next course, the Divination Lab, you'll do all the steps up to this point and then insert a divination technique and take it for a test drive!

Don't worry, only a few more lessons and you'll be ready to hop into the lab and run your hands lovingly over your oracle cards.

(Wasn't that the easiest class ever? You're done for the Night and you still have time to moon gaze or look for meteor showers!)

Lesson 6:

RECORD THE RESULTS

Divinations can be incredibly fleet-footed, Firefly. They race through your consciousness and just as quickly disappear back into the shadows of the subconscious. In order to interpret their messages you have to coax them into lingering. Below are my favorite techniques for capturing and recording oracular images. These techniques will work for both visualized journeys and dreams.

* Before entering a divination, make a conscious decision to remember what you see. Repeat this intention to yourself, either out loud or in your head. Three is the magic number for this type of repetition (see if researching *numerology* will tell you why!).

* Put your journal—with a pen marking the page where you've already written your question—within easy reach.

* When you surface from your vision or dream, keep your eyes closed. Replay the images on your eyelids, mentally adding words to what you are seeing.

* Reach for your journal and start writing. Keep other movements to the minimum. (A trip to the bathroom is treacherous at this phase!)

* Recount your experience in the present tense: *I* am *on a train heading south from a city I don't recognize* instead of *I* was *on a train . . .* Writing in the present tense will give you the sense of reexperiencing the divination instead of recalling it. Reexperiencing will offer up more details than memory will.

Note: Not every type of divination will take you deep into altered consciousness. For readings that fall into the category of amplifying intuition, you'll simply need to record your question and the answers you received.

Homework: Tell It in the Present Tense

Practice recalling events in the present tense by making notes about your day. Remember it's *Oh, sheesh, my coffee is spilling all over my lap* not *I spilled my coffee on my lap.*

Can you see how, in this example, the first takes you further into the experience and you might then record the sensations of having hot coffee in your lap, while the second sentence places you at a distance and does not invite the same sort of sense-related reflection?

WE INTERRUPT OUR REGULARLY
SCHEDULED PROGRAMMING

Tomorrow Night's lesson is on interpreting dreams and divinations. But you need one more puzzle piece before you begin unraveling your divinations: directions to a place called the collective unconscious. So tonight, I'll give you the cosmic GPS coordinates and we'll have class in the C.U. I spend inordinate amounts of starlight perched in a corner of the C.U. Cafe, watching stories unveil themselves and dreams drift past. You probably do, too . . . you just may not know it yet!

You'll be using the collective unconscious both as a divination tool and as an interpretation compendium, so it's an important place to become familiar with. Plus, you never know who you'll run into when you step through its doors.

It's easy to join me at the C.U. Cafe: you simply need to soften your gaze or close your eyes, and relax your rational mind. If you've lit candles so you can do your Night School lessons by their glow, you may want to blow them out before you step out of linear time. Once in the collective unconscious you won't be wholly in the physical world to tend to them.

Ready to go?

Soften your gaze or close your eyes. Take a few breaths, allowing each to go deeper than the one before. Allow the image of the marble front steps of a magnificent library to appear in your mind's eye. Walk up the steps to the portico and look up to see the ceiling vaulted with stars. The doors are tall and arched, swinging smoothly outward when your hand touches the curved brass handle. Inside, the floor is shushed with warm carpets, revealing the designs of a thousand weavers. If you're not in a hurry, pause and admire their work before peeking into stacks crafted from rare rosewood and lined with books. The oldest are stored spine in and their titles are penned on the edge of their pages. Some are leather, some cloth. The air smells like vetiver and maritime pine. It's okay to gawk. I do, every single time.

There's a live wood desk just ahead, the trunk growing horizontal to the floor for a stretch before twisting gracefully upward to fill the cupola. My day-brain always finds it incongruous to see a computer resting on this leafed and living surface, but my Night-mind has never needed the collective consciousness to eschew technology. The infinite isn't necessarily ancient.

When you get to the librarian's desk, check in, head around the center tree, and veer to the left. It won't be long before you'll begin to catch the twin scents of hot ambrosia and coffee. Just follow your nose: the cafe is through the second archway. You'll see me at a high-top in the back, just past the table of boisterous boys debating ancient Egyptian symbolism. Get a drink, pull up a stool, and I'll tell you why I've pulled you into this cosmic interspace.

The collective unconscious is where, you'll remember from lesson 9 of your Foundations course, the threads of the world converge—which means it's a place in which you can begin to suss out how things are connected. It's also where we, collectively, store the symbols and myths that fuel our imagination, dreams, and divinations. Interestingly, the collective unconscious is not culturally specific; it is instead the wellspring, the fount of imagination and metaphor, that provides the images and symbols utilized by all human cultures—which is why, back in the material realm, you'll see symbolism replicated across civilizations that have had little contact with each other.

Are you beginning to see why access to the collective unconscious might be useful for interpreting your divinations?

It's important to note that the collective unconscious is not the same as the subconscious, which you're probably more intimately familiar with: the subconscious is the place within yourself where unacknowledged thoughts and feelings hide out, waiting for you to notice them. Sometimes those thoughts and feelings creep up on your conscious mind, fluttering through your peripheral awareness or darting in unexpectedly to wreak havoc on your otherwise orderly world. Your subconscious is likely responsible for an uncomfortable meal during which you blurted out a truth your dinner partner didn't want to hear or your seemingly out-of-the-blue decision to quit your job . . . *right now*. The subconscious is a private and personal space, while the collective unconscious is a universal portal open to everyone, regardless of race, creed, color, sexual orientation.

Homework: Research a Symbol

Choose a symbol that you're fond of, for example, a raven or spiral.

Research this symbol's meaning across multiple cultures. Head to your computer, open a web browser, and try typing in the symbol plus the name of a culture (like *raven + Celtic, raven + Cherokee, raven + Egyptian, raven + Japanese*).

First, notice whether your chosen symbol appears in a multiplicity of cultural myths, folklores, designs, and sacred rites.

Next, compare how your symbol is used across cultures. Can you find the thread of the collective unconscious running through the symbol you chose? Can you see the universal traits of your symbol woven through a diversity of individual cultural appearances?

Now think about why you chose this symbol. What does it mean in your life and experience? Can you see the collective unconscious running through your own thoughts?

INTERPRET YOUR DIVINATION

For divinations that appear in your mind as images and symbols, inter-pretation is as important as the original divining. But it's your Night-brain doing this work, Firefly. It's not logical or necessarily rational. You might find yourself making sideways associations. For instance, a raven might make you think of Edgar Allan Poe, which makes you think of the 11th grade literature class in which you read "Annabel Lee" and sat behind a girl whose hair curled in spirals like the midnight blue tattoos of Celtic warriors. Not only is it okay to follow these free associations, it's necessary to pull on the threads to see where they lead.

(A surprising number of things connect with each other if you let them, Firefly. Whoever said "the universe is a giant web of spider silk" was on to something.)

Your innate connection to the collective unconscious gives you the internal library of images and symbols you'll need to begin your interpre-tations. You can start this process by using the exercise from your home-work in the last lesson.

Take notice, Firefly: I said that you can use your connection to the col-lective unconscious to *begin* your interpretation. How, you might wonder, do you end it?

Solid interpretation skills come not just from understanding universal symbolism. They come from pairing universal symbolism with knowledge of how you yourself think, because *you* are the lens through which the divination or dream is being viewed. Let's look more closely at how you might proceed in interpreting your divination after you've considered the universal meanings.

There are plenty of books that list broad interpretations of common symbols. These books will often say things like:

* *bat*: bats represent fear. If bats are flying overhead, you are generically fearful, but if they are tangled in your hair, they represent a specific fear.

* *blue*: the color blue is calming and tranquil. It often represents water.

* *box*: a dream about boxes indicates an imminent move, so pack up!

But what if you've been studying bats since you were eight and find them beautiful and fascinating? Or you were wearing a blue dress the morning your grandpa died? Or your favorite saying is "think outside the box"?

When it comes to understanding your divinations, you need to remember that *your* perception is the lens through which you make your interpretation. You can use a web search or symbol dictionary as a jumping-off point, but, ultimately, your personal history and predilections need to be added if the cake is going to rise.

So the steps of divination and dream work interpretation are:

* Divine or dream.

* Visit a book or consult the internet to explore universal meanings, remembering that the universal meaning lies at the crossroads of the various individual interpretations.

* Add in the special sauce of your personal experience and perception.

P.S. If you're interpreting another person's divination, you will need to know how they think and how various symbols resonate within their psyche. This is best achieved by asking them questions about the symbols that have popped up in their divination or dream—so if they had monkeys appear in a dream you could ask *Do you have memories of monkeys from your childhood?* or offer them multiple possible interpretations to see which resonates: *I wonder if the monkeys are about relaxing and feeling a little freer in your life. Or maybe you feel as if you're being treated like a monkey?* Gentle pondering will often get someone talking, and after they get talking, they'll usually find their way to their own interpretation.

Homework: Practice Reading Symbols

Pull out your journal. Work on interpreting the symbolism of these four things, beginning with history and mythology, then looking at modern scientific and/or engineering information, moving on to take a gander at known symbolism, and ending with your personal reflection on how these symbols resonate through the lens of *you.*

* **An Owl**
* **A Diamond**
* **A Rowan Tree**
* **A Circular Staircase**

Extra Credit

Ponder this: Can you actively imagine a visit to the C.U. Library to research an archetype or symbol without your own subconscious joining the party? That is, is it possible for you to get an unbiased look at the collective unconscious?

Lesson 8:

DON YOUR SAFETY GOGGLES!

Real talk, Firefly:

Inter-spirit space travel can be a wee bit dangerous.

Why?

First, you're traveling beyond your usual state of consciousness. Even the possibility of this type of journey is glorious, mysterious, and thrilling. So thrilling, in fact, that the idea of returning to make dinner and watch TV feels like a poor trade for flying by griffin-back or having tea with Marie Antoinette.

But the point of the journey is the return. Religious anthropologist Mircea Eliade tells of a Siberian shaman crossing the rainbow bridge to visit the world of spirit. This is always a two-way trip: the shaman travels to the higher realms and then returns with information and teachings to share. The whole point of the journey is to carry back this wisdom. So always pack your visitor's visa, an empty suitcase you can fill with souvenirs, and your round-trip ticket when you travel to the collective unconscious.

Where exactly are you going when you visit the collective unconscious? Is this a spiritual realm like the place the Siberian shaman visited? Is it an inner realm, second star from your subconscious? Do these distinctions even matter?

I like to think of our consciousness like a doughnut, Firefly. Your day consciousness is the doughy goodness on the outside. Your subconscious and the collective unconscious exist in the hole.

Is the hole inside the doughnut or outside the doughnut? Can the hole exist without the doughnut?

Better minds than mine have contemplated this since before the existence of doughnuts.

But here's what I know:

Whether you think of the hole as outside or inside, it's a portal you want to approach with respect. There are energies there that will challenge your ideas and ethics. In various religions, these energies might be called demons or devils. In Jungian psychology, these are the shadow archetypes—the less-civilized side of your own proclivities. In more modern spiritual terms, we might refer to them as negative energy. Whatever words you choose, you want to approach these challenging energies consciously and intentionally. When you enter the collective unconscious, you want to bring your sense of right and wrong, and your sense of self, with you.

Different cultures, religions, and spiritual practices have found ways to filter what comes through the portal: there are dream and spirit catchers, a circle of salt cast on the ground, and wreaths of holly. There's the vesica piscis—a symbol with two overlapping circles arranged like an ancient Venn diagram—which guards the lid on the Chalice Well at Glastonbury. All of these turn the hole into a door.

And a door doesn't just open. It has hinges with which to close it.

So when you visit the collective unconscious, you will want to imagine a door, which you can open when you arrive and then close behind you. Use the same door to go in as you do to go out. If you practice with the visualization I gave you on page 113, then the arched doorway into the library of the C.U. can become your door. Or you might find another visualization that suits you better.

Making a habit of clearly separating the worlds of the collective unconscious and your everyday reality is good for your sanity, so there are rituals of entry and departure that we teach all first-year students at the Night School.

When you are ready to travel to the C.U.—meaning the question you want to ask is prepared and your journal is laid out ready to receive the answers—pick up your compass. Since compasses have been used for both divination and direction, at the Night School we carry our compass with us when we journey to the collective unconscious so we remain grounded and don't get lost.

Imagine approaching the door of the collective unconscious. Are you on a path? Walking up stairs? Riding a star-scooter across the Night sky? As you draw near, repeat the question that you are heading into the C.U. to research. You can say it aloud or in your mind. Step through the door and into the collective unconscious . . .

And you'll receive instructions on what to do next in the Waking Dream Lab next semester!

But meanwhile, know that you will take your compass with you into the C.U. and hold it in your hand as a reminder of the path to return to ordinary consciousness. In addition, you will exit the collective uncon-scious through the same door you entered and you'll be sure to shut that door behind you when you leave.

To reiterate, Firefly, you have three tips to help you separate your every-Night consciousness from the waking dream of the C.U.:

(1) **Carry your compass (so you don't get lost!).**

(2) **Enter and exit through the same doorway.**

(3) **Close the door behind you.**

Now that you know how to get there and back safely, let's talk about the second peril of divination: giving up your sense of self and your free will.

Astrology, oracle cards, and waking dreams are tools for stepping into the collective unconscious. They act as reminders that your life is arche-typical and mythic. The collective unconscious is a place to find guid-ance which you then interpret, analyze, and decide how to apply to your life. When you encounter archetypes in the C.U., meet them as an equal, remembering that while they can offer you knowledge of the inner realms, you have experience of the outer world and the intricacies of everyday life. If divination sends your free will to the sidelines, it's time to rethink how you're approaching it.

Divinations are signposts on your trail. They can offer you peace and a moment of connection, or they can jar you into reassessing everything you thought you believed. Whenever you're charting paths for your future self, or learning something new about yourself and your life—whether you learn it from a doctor, a teacher, your astrologer, or a deck of oracle cards—you have the creative challenge of figuring out how to work with that new information, deciding how it will enrich, instead of inhibit, your life choices.

When challenges and obstacles are pointed out, you get to choose how they're going to impact you. Are you going to let them stop you in your tracks, or will they make you stretch and grow and get wily as you work your way past them? Remember, divination is one tool of many. When you have a query about the future, approach it from a variety of angles, then compile the information you've gotten—both practical and spiritual. Guidance is not a dictatorship, and if in the course of a waking or Nighttime dream you're asked to give up autonomy, know you're encountering one of those challenging, devilish archetypes which indicates that it's time for your free will to step up instead of step out.

A few other tips on the art of divination before you head to the labs:

* Choose the variety of divination that matches your question. Is it a yes/no question? Then a pendulum might do the trick. Is it a question that needs an understanding of a huge chunk of your life and the patterns that go along with it? Then you should probably book an appointment with your trusty astrologer.

* Don't ask the same question seven times just because you don't like the answer. (Do you like it when someone keeps asking you the same question hoping for a different reply?) If you realize your initial question was unclear, carefully formulate additional questions for clarification.

* While you don't want to keep asking the same question, it's fabulous to keep questioning the answer! Sit with your interpretation and see how you feel about it over time. Dream on it and see if it feels right. Write about it and notice where your thoughts lead you. Be aware of your biases and proclivities and give yourself space to observe how they are affecting your interpretation.

And now . . . it's time for a little pause. (More about that after Additional Semester Readings and Resources!)

Enjoy your semester break, and I will see you for Divination Labs next week.

ADDITIONAL READINGS AND RESOURCES

While Carl Jung is credited with naming the collective unconscious, it bears a striking resemblance to a construct that existed long before Jung. In addition to reading Jung's *Letters*, backtrack and check out Plato's theory of forms. (Reading all of *The Republic* is probably unnecessary, Firefly. Because studying Plato's forms is a component of most first year philosophy classes, you'll find plenty of online study guides that discuss this philosophy.)

If you're curious about other ways in which humans have conceptualized a realm of shared image and symbol, visit *Dante's Inferno* for a quick trip to Hell. Now here's where it gets interesting, Firefly: compare *The Inferno* with the ancient Sumerian text of *The Journey of Inanna* from 2112 BCE. (You don't need a book for this one: you'll find translations online.) Finally, consult accounts of shamanism in the Siberian steppes and the journeys to Dreamtime of the Indigenous peoples of Australia. Look at the spirit travels of the Yup'ik of Alaska and the soul flights of the Yaskomo and of the Wai-Wai people of Northern Brazil. What common threads do you see? After doing this research, are you a yea or nay on Jung's assertion that symbols are universal?

If you want easy-to-read explorations of Jung's theories, spend some time with Robert Johnson. Both *Inner Work* and *Owning Your Own Shadow* are thought-provoking without being dense. *Inner Work* aligns with the concepts in this course, while *Owning Your Own Shadow* might rightfully belong in the Mysteries of Being Human library.

To begin to untangle the threads between how our minds receive words versus our relationship with images, *The Alphabet Versus the Goddess* by Leonard Shlain is thick as pea soup but infinitely more fascinating.

To meet some of the characters and archetypes you'll find in the collective unconscious, read books of fairy tales and myths and check out Kim Krans's *The Wild Unknown Archetypes* book and deck.

If you're intrigued with the idea of the Doctrine of Signatures, Liz Gilbert's book *The Signature of All Things* works with the concept in novel form.

Reading the human body—whether it's the lines on the palm or the face or a zillion other small signs you never suspected—is infinitely enlightening. The best compendium of information I have found is in *Reading the Body: Ohashi's Book of Oriental Diagnosis* by Tom Monte and Wataru Ohashi.

Finally, if you want to truly understand the importance of asking the right question, take a spin through Douglas Adams's *Hitchhiker's Guide to the Galaxy*, paying close attention to chapter 28.

Extra, Extra Credit

Ask yourself this important question: do you really want extra, extra credit or do you just want to get to the Divination Labs?

semester break

IT'S A WRAP, FIREFLY!

Congratulations on completing your first semester at the Night School.

Correspondence students—that's you!—often forget to rest. But brains need downtime in order to assimilate new information. Give yourself a moment to have a cup of tea. Walk outside and have a chat with Orion or Cassiopeia. Percolate on everything you've learned and wondered about.

It's time to nap, rest, and digest. (And if you're really not at all tired, you can head to the Night Library at the back of the book to find some extracurricular reading material.)

But don't just charge ahead: you'll be doing yourself a disservice. Over the years, I've noticed that positive learning outcomes are often associated with a good, solid pause. So take time to assimilate. Let your learning simmer: I promise it will come together to form a rich and tasty soup!

Your homework for the next week is to wander aimlessly down the pathways of the Night and track down the meaning of any symbols or archetypes that dare to cross your path. If you don't feel like strolling, invite Serendipity to tea; she's always up for a cuppa.

Your second semester begins a week from this evening. (Mark the date in your calendar!) Before you begin again, make time for a midterm check-in: I want to see how you're doing!

Meanwhile, if you haven't yet, gather your supplies for Semester 2:

Supply List for Semester 2

* a rattle
* a pendulum
* an herb bundle
* a tarot or oracle deck
* a scrying mirror
* ingredients for Bananas Foster
* an ephemeris
* a star map

This is one of my favorite moments, Firefly: pull up a chair so I can prep you for your second semester at the Night School! I hope it's going well for you so far and that you're remembering to breathe spaciousness into your studies.

While Tools of the Mystic, your next course and Divination Lab, is both enticing and enchanting, it's also a class that can be particularly aggravating to your everyday consciousness. It's likely your day-brain has been trained to see divination and dream work as an elaborate charade even though they're as real as the moon to your Night-brain. This difference sets up a dissonance, a friction if you will, that can rub a divination the wrong way.

It's okay to have conflicted feelings. Remember, what's important is that you *know* how you feel, not that you *control* how you feel.

I want to provide some fodder that might tempt your recalcitrant day-brain to join in the divination feast! What I'm going to recommend is a bit like the *Step Outside Yourself* exercise we did in Mysteries of Being Human (see page 70). The first step is to acknowledge your day-brain's reticence. Observe your thoughts without judging them. (Thoughts tend to duck for cover when you get judgy with them, Firefly!) Then try having a conversation with your day-brain that goes something like this:

I know the work we're doing here is a little sideways of your good sense. Still, I was hoping to get you at least nominally on board with our explorations. I don't need full buy-in; just a willingness to try something new.

I want to provide a little historical context to sate your sensibilities. You see, the idea that there are multiple ways of knowing is not simply New Age or Night School. The great Albert Einstein is often quoted as calling intuition a sacred gift, and Steve Jobs, founder of Apple, was clear that there would be no Mac without it.

So how did we get trained to be anti-intuition? When did the Night become a second-class citizen?

Remember being perched on an orange plastic-molded chair in elementary school, Mr. Landis delivering lessons as though what he was saying was *THE TRUTH?* He never interrupted a history lesson to dramatically whisper: *This is not the only truth! But we're going to go with it for a moment and we'll explore some other types of truth later on.*

I think it all started then. We became convinced that truth was singular.

But what if there are many ways of knowing and multiple paths to truth?

From what I've seen, the professional thinkers of the world are constantly rearranging the puzzle pieces, trying to figure out how our human minds work. The existence of less-than-usual ways of receiving information, like the ones used for divining or dreaming, is not a newfangled concept. While not popular in most industrialized societies, intuitive knowing has long been a part of the compendium of human knowledge. In fact, for many cultures not as touched by industrialization—like those indigenous to Australia, many parts of the Americas, and Africa—intuitive knowing is still, as Einstein named it, a sacred gift.

Divination is, at its heart, a form of intuitive knowing.

Is there any chance, day-brain, that you would agree to see it as a sacred gift, and marvel at it, even if you don't understand it?

A conversation like this creates space for what the poet Samuel Coleridge called a willing "suspension of disbelief," which I like to think of as a pocket of null space within which you can perform the experiments of divination without doubt clouding the lens.

Remember: the Night does not require your thoughts to march in rational formation. However, you need to be aware enough to name your inner turmoil. I call mine Cassandra.

Alright, Firefly, it's time for Semester 2!

Diving into Divination,
Bea

Oh! Before you dive in, spend a moment with your journal. Write down three things you learned last semester and how these three revelations will influence you going forward.

SEMESTER 2

WE'RE BACK, FIREFLY!

This next semester has some of our most intriguing classes: Tools of the Mystic (your Divination Lab), Elemental Alchemization, and, finally, Harnessing the Celestial Tides.

You'll begin in the Divination Labs, where you'll get hands-on experience with the process of scrying, which you studied in Divining the Night last semester. Especially if you've always gone to an astrologer or had your tarot cards read, this is your chance to have a direct experience of divination. Here at the Night School we recommend you sample all the flavors before selecting your favorite, so grab a spoon and dig in!

Next up is Elemental Alchemization which, appropriately (I think!), starts in the kitchen. (This is a very tasty semester, Firefly!) We'll work to understand the rather convoluted history of the four elements so you can use them as ingredients in all your future mystical workings.

Finally, you'll fly into Harnessing the Celestial Tides, which covers the history and basics of astrology . . . and includes an airplane ride! (Because even I couldn't find an available rocket ship on such short notice.)

Pack your divination tools, your apron, and your compass, and let's launch into Semester 2!

tools of the mystic

(Divination Lab)

ROLL UP YOUR SLEEVES AND DON YOUR SAFETY GOGGLES, Firefly: it's time to do some much-anticipated divination experiments!

As we prepare to begin, just for a moment, imagine that I've given you a new set of kitchen knives. (I know. It's odd for me to be giving you knives, but play along for a few seconds . . .) The knives are the kind that come in a wooden block that sits on the counter and provides you with many more knives than you'll ever use.

All the knives in your new knife block will cut, but after using them to prepare a number of meals, you'll end up realizing that it's easier to cut onions with the smooth chef's knife than the serrated bread knife. Over time, you'll end up with knives that are your personal favorites, and you'll understand the strengths and weaknesses of each of these tools. And remember, your chosen knife for slicing veggies might not be the knife you're "supposed" to use for dicing cucumbers and bell peppers. Give yourself permission to put aside expectations and move toward the tools that are comfortable in your hands, even if they make no sense to anyone else.

One mistake I see students making is trying to master *all* the tools of the Night. Imagine what a mess your kitchen would be if you insisted on using every single blade in that 14-knife set! Just like a chef's knife and a santoku will both make quick work of a tomato, the tools in each of the categories laid out in Divining the Night accomplish similar things, but in slightly different ways. You don't need to master all of them. You instead need to discover those that speak to you and then get good at using them. After choosing your favorites, your time will be best spent developing expertise in a few divining modalities so that you understand the quirks and nuances of each.

While the lab experiments laid out here are specifically designed to partner with your divination course, many of the tools reviewed are multi-functional. As you choose your favorites, be sure to review the other uses, which will be listed at the end of each lab exercise.

Finally, learning to read signs, cards, or dreams is often about letting your vision go fuzzy and allowing yourself to unsee what you've been taught. By doing this, you open yourself up to new truths and possibilities, and enter the place where your inner wisdom dwells. You may not have words for what your body knows, so sink into the sensations. Find the calm surety that comes from gut knowledge and heart wisdom. Step into stillness so you can feel what's right for you. Move your attention from your mind down into your heart. Don't ask yourself what you think; ask yourself what you feel. This is Night-work, so be sure to do this after the sun has set.

And now it's time to get your hands dirty: welcome to the Divination Labs!

SYLLABUS

Dust off your divination tools, Firefly! It's time for Tools of the Mystic, your Divination Laboratory.

In the lessons to come, you'll find suggestions for things you need to actually *try*, not just read or think about. The learning will come from the doing and the experimenting; the words on the page will merely be a guide to help you get started.

Try each form of divination at least once. Often it takes a few tries to get comfortable enough to know whether a particular form resonates with your personal soul stuff. Experiment with the experiment, tweaking it so it works for you—just like wriggling into a new pair of moon boots and squishing around 'til the foam conforms to your foot.

As you test-drive each form of divining, keep the following notations in your journal so you can track your results:

* **Type of divination.**

* **Moon phase you are currently in.**

* **Question asked at the beginning of the divination.**

* **Notes about the quality of the question: Did you feel like this was a useful question? What did you learn about yourself or your question?**

* **How did you feel afterward? Were your personal stars polished or dimmed by performing this particular divination? Do you feel shiny and empowered or dull and lackluster?**

* **Give your divination a rating on the five-star scale.**

A few other tidbits to keep in your Night-mind: try to attend each lab listed below so you can experience the multiplicity of magics. This is not because you will continue using each and every one of them, but because you won't know which divination tools you prefer until you experiment.

These are your Divination Labs and the types of divining you will experience:

EXPERIMENT 1:	Show Me Yes—using a pendulum
EXPERIMENT 2:	By the Smoke—using smoke
EXPERIMENT 3:	Write It Out—using pen and paper
EXPERIMENT 4:	Oneiromancy—using dreams
EXPERIMENT 5:	The Waking Dream—using active imagination
EXPERIMENT 6:	What the Cards Say—using images
EXPERIMENT 7:	Peering into the Scrying Mirror—using reflection
EXPERIMENT 8:	Reading the Leaves . . . Or the Bones . . . Or the Stones—using objects to find patterns

More than ever, Firefly, you'll want to do one lab exercise per Night. Give yourself the gift of space to expand the experiments and go deep with each divination tool. Try each tool out in various ways so you can see what suits you and ignites your intuition. And don't forget to run through lessons 1 to 4 from Divining the Night before each divination lab!

Experiment 1:
SHOW ME YES

Let's start with using a pendulum. This is a way of amplifying your Clair and making the unseen visible. Pendulums work well for yes/no questions.

A pendulum is part of the dowser's tool kit. Traditionally, it was held over a map as a way of finding the rough location of something like gold or water. The dowser would then go to the site and use dowsing rods to zero in on the exact locale.

You can use a pendulum designed specifically for this purpose or any small bob that you can hang on a string or chain, like a button on a thread, a key on a cord, or a bolt on a string. A necklace with a charm can also work beautifully.

Thread the string or chain through the bob, and then hold both ends together so you don't have a knot on top affecting the balance.

Hold the string so the pendulum swings free. Some people sit with their elbow balanced on their leg and the pendulum swinging between their knees. I hold the pendulum in my right hand and let it swing over my left hand which I hold flat (like I'm giving a dog a treat). Try some different positions and see what's comfortable for you.

Begin your session by asking the pendulum to show you yes. It may swing clockwise, counterclockwise, or back and forth.

Then ask your pendulum to show you no. Notice the difference between a yes and a no. For some people, the pendulum doesn't move at all when the answer is no.

You're now ready to ask your question and record your results.

Note whether your pendulum makes any movements other than the yes or no that you established. Track those movements over time and see if they are indicating that the outcome of your question doesn't matter or that you're not asking a particularly good question.

Also notice the velocity of the swing. My pendulum sometimes feels like the Earth orbiting the sun, gaining a certain gravity and zest in a way that I interpret as "heck yes!"

OTHER USES FOR A PENDULUM:

You can use your pendulum over a map or a picture of your home to help you locate lost objects.

By using imagery, you can ask more complex questions than a simple yes or no. For instance, if you were choosing between two rental apartments, you could hold your pendulum over a photo of each to get a positive or negative impression.

Experiment 2:

BY THE SMOKE

Divination by smoke is called *capnomancy*. It's been used for predicting both the long-term future (like *is war coming?*) and the short-term future (like *is it safe to camp here?*). At the Night School, we use it to make the invisible visible so we can more easily see the patterns swirling around a specific person, which will give you hints about their past, present, and future.

You'll need a bundle of dried and burnable plant material. (Please see the note on burning herbs in your supply list on page 12, Firefly, before you light up!) You'll also want something fireproof to hold beneath your plant bundle to catch the ashes. Your bundle should be two to four inches long, half an inch to an inch wide, and loosely packed so that oxygen—which is necessary for fire—can circulate. Bigger is "fire hazard," not "better."

Smoke is best suited to questions about a person: it is a way of gathering additional information by helping you see things your daylight eyes don't notice. The person will need to be present and willing to work with you, so this is not good for long-distance divinations. Consider working with smoke as a doorway into both your own intuition and a conversation.

As always, start with your question. For example, *What is contributing to my friend's sleeplessness?*

Light your herb bundle and then tamp it down so it's smoldering. Trace your friend's outline, about a foot from their body, with the smoldering bundle, letting the smoke swirl around them. Watch how the smoke flows: Is it moving from low to high? Left to right? Vice versa?

Does it swirl or thicken anywhere? Skitter away from their heart or right knee? Curl in for a snuggle? See how it moves: flowing, not flowing; thinning, thickening.

Now begin asking additional questions of your subject based on your observations, like:

> **I see the smoke is thick over your left shoulder. Do you feel like you're carrying something? What do you think it is? What does it feel like?**

Ask the questions that come to your mind, even if they seem silly. The smoke is facilitating a connection with your intuition in order to help you help your friend figure out what's going on.

You can also work with smoke to see the patterns swirling around yourself! Simply stand in front of a full-length mirror. Do you carry stress in your neck: how is the smoke reacting there? How's the smoke responding when you hold it over your giving hand (your dominant hand) vs. your receiving hand? What does the smoke confirm or make you curious about?

OTHER USES FOR SMOKE:

You can use smoke to shift the energy in your home by lighting and tamping your bundle in the same way, then walking through your space. Move clockwise to build energy, like when your space feels blah and tired, and counterclockwise to unwind energy, like when you've had a fight with your partner and need to, quite literally, clear the air.

Experiment 3:

WRITE IT OUT

Sometimes simply asking yourself the question will lead to the answer you need!

Use freewriting to connect with your own intuition and find words for the information your subconscious is constantly recording about the world around you.

The process couldn't be easier, Firefly:

* **Grab your notebook, turn to a blank page, and write your question at the top.**

* **Set a timer for 10 minutes or put on some music and write for three songs (a song is usually about three to four minutes long).**

* **Take a few deep breaths of the Night air and let your eyes go soft.**

* **Then start writing! The goal is to keep your pen moving across the page, even if you feel like you're writing nonsense.**

In fact, I can pretty much guarantee that you'll feel silly or lost or confused for at least the first three minutes. You'll feel like you are making things up or that you don't know what to write.

Keep writing, even if the words don't seem to make sense. Just write anything that comes into your head—including "I don't know what to write! This is stupid!" At a certain point, your ego will step aside . . . and that's when the magic happens!

OTHER USES FOR FREEWRITING:

Writing is a fabulous tool for connection! If you want to connect with a plant, animal, crystal, or even one of your ancestors, ask it/them/him/her to share, then let your hand flow across the page. Don't worry about making sense of your writing: write first, interpret later.

Experiment 4:

ONEIROMANCY

Oneiromancy is a fancy word for using dreams as a method of divination. It goes back eons: in 3000 BCE the Mesopotamian kings were minding (and mining!) their dreams; a few thousand years later, a Greco-Roman dream book called the *Oneirocritica* showed us that dream work was still alive and well; and another thousand years later, the Japanese courtier Sei Shonagon waded through her dreams in *The Pillow Book*. Oneiromancy and the desire to explore the dreamscape are universal.

The setup for oneiromancy is simple, but don't let that fool you. Dreams are slippery, and learning to catch them with your bare hands takes practice and persistence.

Here's your deceptively simple arrangement for dream divination:

* Place your journal and a pen on your nightstand, within easy reach.

* Before going to sleep, sit on the edge of your bed. Take a few deep breaths with your feet flat on the floor. Set your question in your mind, with the intention that you will dream on it and remember your dream.

* When you wake up, stay very still so you don't scare your dream away.

* Replay what you remember of your dream while your eyes are still closed, moving the dream from image to words in your mind.

* When you feel like you've caught it, reach for your journal. Try to keep your movements minimal. Don't even turn on the light.

* Begin writing. List big ideas and images first so you don't lose them, then go back and write the dream as a story. Use the first-person present tense (*I am walking through a moonlit garden* instead of *she walked through a moonlit garden*).

This is the first step. The next step is interpretation, which we went over in Divining the Night (p. 116). Remember, interpreting is just as important as dreaming!

Record your dreams for a few weeks and see what comes to you. If you're having trouble remembering your dreams, mugwort is a traditional aid. The tea isn't tasty, but try a few sips before bed or burn some mugwort incense before you fall asleep.

> ## OTHER WAYS OF WORKING WITH DREAMS:
> If you want a self-study project, Firefly, dive into lucid dreaming to enhance your Night-life!

Experiment 5:

THE WAKING DREAM

In order to know yourself and begin to suss out the patterns at play in your life, you need some me-time in the underworld of the collective unconscious. Some visit the C.U. every Night in dreams, but not everyone can remember their adventures in the morning. The waking dream is the perfect option for finding your way into the doughnut hole on your own time, and since you'll be wide awake, you can note down your experiences more easily than when coming back from Nighttime dreams.

A waking dream is an act of purposeful imagining. You may feel like you're making up the images you're seeing. Since that's *exactly* what you need to do to get a waking dream going, when you feel like you're "making it up" know that you're on the right track!

The trick is to allow that purposeful beginning to slide into softness, to stop steering the boat of your consciousness and instead let it drift. Especially if you're a person who's used to making things happen, it can be frustrating to wait and see what's next. Essentially, you'll be opening the door to the C.U. and then waiting in the foyer hoping some library assistant or wandering goddess takes pity on you. As you wait, allow yourself to grow softer and softer so that you are 100 percent in your non-judgy Night-brain.

Follow these steps into the altered state of consciousness of the waking dream:

* As always, prepare your question and jot it onto a fresh page in your journal.

* Then prep your space: choose some soothing music, create a cozy nest where you won't be disturbed, and get your compass.

* Set a timer to go off, softly, in 20 minutes.

* Get comfy and be sure you're holding your compass. Imagine yourself approaching the door of the collective unconscious. Be specific with the details: what does this path look and smell like? What sounds do you hear? Are you walking or riding on something? Repeat the question you are carrying with you as you step through your imagined door and into the foyer of the collective unconscious. (The first few times you do this, your visualizations will likely vary. Over time you'll establish imagery for yourself that you'll always use to begin your dreaming.)

* Settle into the foyer of the C.U. and see what sparks your intuition and imagination. Keep your compass in your hand. Allow your mind to relax and go soft. Let your shoulders ease and your facial muscles rest.

* At some point, your inner vision will take over . . . and it's hard to say exactly what will happen next!

Enjoy your adventures until your timer rings. When it does, work your way back to the C.U. foyer and step through the tall, arched doors to exit, remembering to close them behind you. Lock the door between your every-Night consciousness and the C.U. Retrace your route back to consciousness, moving toward the image of your physical self. Fully inhabit your own skin by wriggling your fingers and toes and taking a few deep breaths.

Just like a sleeping dream, you now need to work on interpreting what you envisioned. Remember to write your journal notes in the first person, present tense. Get all your notes down before you use the skills you learned in Divining the Night to begin to read the patterns of your waking dream.

> **OTHER USES OF THE WAKING DREAM:**
> Jungian therapists and those who have done neo-shamanic studies use variations on the waking dream. Often called journeying or journey work, this type of exploration can be used to identify spirit guides and to recover lost parts of yourself—a practice known as soul retrieval.

Experiment 6:

WHAT THE CARDS SAY

The oldest surviving tarot set, known as the Visconti-Sforza deck, was created for the Duke of Milan's family around 1440. The images on the cards were inspired by popular Carnival costumes, and the cards were used for a game called *tarocchi*, which was similar to the modern-day game of bridge. In the 18th century, as a wave of occultism swept through Europe, the tarot deck became popular as a divination tool, and all sorts of books were published attempting to link the deck to ancient Egypt or the Jewish Kabbalah.

But the true source of the cards is perfect for how we use them at the Night School, Firefly, because the original cards were created based on the outfits worn during Carnival. Just as today's Halloween costumes represent the archetypes currently at play in our culture, the Carnival costumes represented the archetypes that were relevant in mid-millennia Europe. Those archetypes, drawn from classical literature, religion, and the depths of the human psyche, are still a part of the collective unconscious today. The use of these archetypes and images provides us with a hall pass straight into the C.U.

Using cards will help your mind somersault into free association, letting you see situations with fresh eyes. When you're feeling unclear or unsure, the cards offer an unexpected filter and a different perspective. It's kind of like having a good friend or therapist who asks questions out of left field, to get you thinking in a whole new way. The images present on your cards, and the words offered in the tiny booklet that likely accompanied them, will help you slip from the confines of your day-brain.

Don't have a deck? No problem. The lovely thing about how we use the cards at the Night School is that they're easily replaced by other sources of imagery, like the illustrations on the pages of a book or photos you've cut from a magazine or printed from your computer. Using a book for divination is called bibliomancy, and it's very simple to do: at the point in the instructions below where you would draw a card, instead open an illustrated book to a random page.

How to divine with images:

* **As always, it starts with your question. Wait until your question has crystallized and feels clear to you, then write it in your notebook.**

* **When your question is ready, hold your deck (or book, or pile of images) between your hands, with the back side facing up. Breathe in and out, allowing yourself to come to center, then imagine your question infusing your hands, bathing the cards in the energy of your query.**

* It's now time to draw a card. There are many ways to do this: you can cut the deck and draw a card off the top, spread the cards back side up and draw whichever feel right, or think of a number and count the cards until you get to your number of choice.

* After you draw your card, you'll move into the interpretation phase of the divination. Remember that everything you're seeing in the card and reading in the tiny booklet relates to your question.

* When interpreting an image, begin by examining it in detail. Notice the colors and whether it contains movement or stillness. Identify the natural elements (Earth, Water, Fire, Air) and how they are represented. Begin noting your observations in your journal, simply writing exactly what you see: *I see a woman in a green dress. She looks sad. Actually, she looks like she's trying to pretend she's happy but I'm not buying it.*

* Now let your mind free-associate. For the example above, I might think: *Green is the color of envy. The woman is pretending not to feel what she is really feeling. Is she feeling envy?* Then apply this to your situation and question: *Hmm, am I pretending a feeling I don't actually feel? Am I envious of someone or something?*

Occasionally your eyes might want to be more involved in the choosing process. Another way to approach the cards is to flip them illustration side up and use your soft Night-gaze to study the pictures, choosing the image that feels intuitively right for you to work with at this moment.

Using the cards stirs the cauldron of the collective unconscious. By seeing what floats to the surface, you gain insight into yourself and the patterns swirling around you. If you think of the cards as illuminating the current constellations of your life, you leave yourself a sky full of free will and plenty of room to pivot on your path.

OTHER USES FOR YOUR CARDS:

Oracle cards and tarot cards are slightly different. Oracle cards are not part of a larger system: each card has a distinct meaning not necessarily related to the rest of the cards in the deck. This makes oracle cards perfectly suited for the manner in which we are using them here.

Tarot, on the other hand, was and is based on the suits found in a deck of playing cards. In the tarot deck, those suits relate to the four elements (which you'll learn more about in your Elemental Alchemization course). Each card is numbered, so the numerological meanings (that's numerology, Firefly) also come into play. On top of that, there's a hierarchy to the cards known as the Major and Minor Arcana, as well as the court cards. Because of all these layers, the tarot cards exist not only as individual meanings, but In relation to one another, weaving a larger tapestry together. The tarot deck is a system and, as such, is perfect for reflecting larger, more systemic, patterns.

A starting place for using your tarot deck to see a bigger picture is to look at the past, present, and future of a situation. For this you'll want to use not just one card, but what we call a spread. The simplest spread is a three-card Past/Present/Future layout, where one card is drawn for the past, a second for the present, and a third for the future. A little research will uncover a plethora of other possible tarot spreads, so match your choice of spread to the type of question you're asking. And remember, as you are reading and interpreting, that the tarot system creates layers of meaning from the elemental, numerical, archetypical, and symbolic so you'll want to look at each card in your spread through a variety of lenses.

Experiment 7:

PEERING INTO THE SCRYING MIRROR

John Dee, mystical adviser to Queen Elizabeth I (that's the Queen Elizabeth from the 16th century, Firefly), was rumored to have a magical disk of polished obsidian—or a "black mirror." In J.R.R. Tolkien's beloved book series The Lord of the Rings, the Mirror of Galadriel was a basin of water pulled fresh from a stream. The stereotypical storefront fortune-teller has a crystal ball swathed in black velvet waiting on her gilded table.

These reflective surfaces are used for scrying (or trying to scry!), which is notoriously difficult. Still, you might find you have a knack for reading messages and guidance through reflection.

I'll lay out a procedure for scrying below. After you've read it through, experiment with different reflective surfaces and see what works for you. There are so many choices:

* mirrors

* polished brass

* crystals

* polished stone

* water

* glass

* fire (Questionable in terms of its reflective qualities, truthfully. I would argue that it's more hypnotic, but people have been scrying the flame for centuries and I suspect they don't care what I think!)

Personally, I find the gentle blur of living water to be best and can occasionally read the water of a creek or river. Experiment with both the natural and the mass-produced, as well as different ways of gazing at the surface. A compact mirror aimed over your left shoulder can produce startling results. Try looking straight on, or alternately, gazing out of the corner of your eye. The combination of reflective surfaces and different ways of viewing will give you a plenitude of possible experiments, Firefly.

Give it a try:

* Work on your question, and when it feels complete, write it on a page in your journal.

* Choose your reflective surface.

* Quiet your thoughts with a few full breaths.

* Hold your question in your mind as you gaze into the reflection.

* Keep your eyes relaxed. Let your mind flow . . . Remember, guidance doesn't come when forced.

* Note what you see in your journal, using the present tense. (Don't overthink it!)

. . . And now it's time for you to interpret what you have seen!

READING THE LEAVES . . . OR THE BONES . . . OR THE STONES

By applying the foundational principle "as above, so below," you can analyze the patterns of small things like tea leaves, bones, sticks, or stones to get a feel for the larger patterns at play. When you use techniques like tasseography (that's a fancy word for reading tea leaves or coffee grounds) or lithomancy (reading stones), you're creating an environment in which patterns and shapes can emerge. And much like scrying, once you choose a subject or problem to focus on, you gain insights from your interpretation of the patterns in relationship to that subject or issue.

Plus, for some, working with patterns will trigger their intuition, allowing them to have insights that extend far beyond the simple patterns in front of them.

As usual, begin with a well-crafted question.

Your exact next step is going to depend on what type of object you've chosen for your reading. Bones, sticks, and stones are usually shaken and thrown. With tea leaves and coffee grounds, the tea or coffee is consumed and the leaves or grounds left at the bottom of the cup are read. Over the long history of divination, people have read everything from oil to flour to ink stains, so don't feel limited to the exact things mentioned here: ask your question and then scatter rice, beans, or spaghetti sticks from your kitchen! The asking of the question and your intention to find the pattern that points toward the answer are the important parts, not the exact tool used.

After the throwing down, the next step is to soften your gaze and look for patterns.

Interpreting these patterns is very similar to how you work with tarot or oracle cards. Before you pull out the book of symbolism, first notice your intuitive hits . . . observe and note down what you see, think, and feel. Remember, Firefly, you're using your Night-brain, allowing things to flow and connect—even if your day-brain is having a conniption fit about wasting perfectly good beans!

ADDITIONAL READINGS AND RESOURCES

In this instance, Firefly, extra reading is actually detrimental: reading keeps you from *doing.* The most productive way to learn to work with your divination tools is to work with your divination tools, over and over again.

Practice makes purple flowers with midnight-blue stamens and a dusting of gold glitter on the leaves . . . as well as all sorts of other images and symbols for you to interpret!

Put down the books and get practicing. The Night needs more purple flowers.

A NOTE BEFORE YOUR NEXT CLASS

Did you know that we do a Cooking Lab at the Night School, Firefly?

We do, and it's scheduled during your next class!

Below is a list of ingredients you'll need to pick up:

* 6 tablespoons butter
* ½ cup brown sugar
* ½ teaspoon ground cinnamon
* 4 bananas
* ¾ cup rum

You may also want a little vanilla ice cream to top it all off. There's something about experiencing the extremes of cold, creamy ice cream and hot, gooey caramel that provides a very convincing argument for finding the perfect, delectable balance of opposite sensations.

See you in the kitchen!

Bea

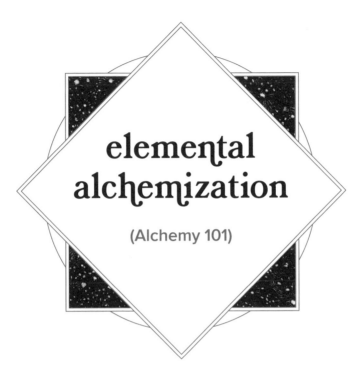

elemental alchemization

(Alchemy 101)

LET'S BEGIN THIS NEXT CLASS BY EXPLORING THE FOUR elements—Earth, Air, Fire, and Water. We'll begin in the kitchen, Firefly. Set the tea water to boil, and while we wait on it, let's have a look around.

The first thing you'll notice is that "Earth" is everywhere, from the onions, potatoes, and lettuce greens to the ceramic mixing bowls and even the wooden spoons you use to scrape the caramelized goodness off the bottom of the sauté pan.

(Yup, your wooden spoon was once a tree and your batter bowl a lump of clay in the ground. Don't forget to notice the objects around you and track them back, not just to the store from which you brought them, but to their true, elemental, origins.)

Earth might be the most obvious of the elements occupying your pantry shelves, but the others live here as well. The heat from your cooktop is Fire, either real or metaphoric, depending on what you use to cook. The flow from your faucet, as well as any other liquids you're concocting with, beautifully demonstrates the properties of Water. And while Air might be the least obvious, it's here, all the same. Look for it in the fizz of your soda, the pockets in your bread loaf, the lift in your whipped cream, and the loft in your soufflé.

While chemistry has declared atoms to be the building blocks of the universe—and therefore also the building blocks of every meal—can you find an atom in your kitchen?

Conceptually, you know they're there. You can wave your hand around vaguely and say, "There are atoms everywhere!" But can you find one and point it out to me so that I, too, can recognize it?

Looking around your kitchen together, it becomes obvious that the four elements are imprinted onto our psyches in ways that atoms and their component parts—protons, neutrons, electrons, and quarks—are not. That imprint also affects language: when someone says, "I'm all fired up!" you know, intuitively, exactly what they mean. You can feel the heat, warmth, and passion they're evoking. If, on the other hand, I were to announce, "I'm all quarked up!" you might have a good gambol *thinking* about it, your brain chasing mine through the subtleties of quarkdom, but on an intuitive level, my statement would *feel* rather meaningless.

The difference between chemistry and alchemy is much the same. As you look around your kitchen and think about the transformations that will occur as you cook, do the letters of the periodic table dance through your brain? Do you explain boiling water to yourself in terms of H_2O excitement or Fire heating Water? Has sitting in the glow of chemistry ever warmed the cockles of your heart while a mug of $C_6H_{12}O_8 + H_2O$ thawed your frozen fingers after a midnight snowball fight?

I think not.

But every time you bake cookies, sauté veggies, or grill up a burger, you're witnessing how Fire transforms Earth. You can stand at the counter and watch your seltzer maker inserting Air into Water. Or, if you've ever made candy, you know that if you add heat (Fire) to the right syrupy concoction, you can evaporate off the liquid (Water) and cool what remains. This bit of elemental alchemy leaves you with the pure, Earthy, sugary goodness we call candy.

In other words, we think about cooking using the language associated with alchemy and the four elements, not the language of chemistry and quarks. And while you've probably never considered it as you fry up an egg for your breakfast, the transformations that take food from raw to cooked are rather spellbinding. Is it any wonder, then, that the Ancient Greek word for cook, *magieros*, shares etymological roots with the word *magic*?

Interestingly, *magieros* is also the word for "priest." What happens, Firefly, if you begin to think of cooking as holy? What if your kitchen is a portal to the same sense of connectedness you feel in the collective unconscious?

(Are you suddenly side-eyeing your kitchen, wondering what it would be like to boil some pasta and marvel at the air bubbles forming as the water heats? Are you curious how it would feel to let your mind soften as the penne somehow—alchemically?—goes from hard to chewy to delicious? Then close your book for the Night. Transform your kitchen into the Sacred Space of the Holy Chef, acolyte to culinary alchemy. Play with your food . . . and the elements! Tomorrow Night you can pick up here with a fresh, zesty, and embodied understanding of the elemental building blocks we're going to discuss.)

This is not the cooking class that I mentioned, Firefly. But your kitchen is a fabulous place to remember that our understanding of the world around us is layered. Having a felt and sensual experience of these layers will help you connect in a way that is more delicious than if you had merely a conceptual, quark-like knowledge of the world around you. Interacting with the alchemy of the four elements offers you a chance to touch the stuff of creation. For this reason, if nothing else, Earth, Air, Fire, and Water hold prominent places in the echelon of the Night. Plus, they're baked into the batter of the collective unconscious in a way that atoms, and their component parts, are not.

SYLLABUS

Elemental Alchemization is a survey course tracing the power of Earth, Air, Water, and Fire from the ancient Greeks to the medieval alchemists, with a quick swing by the writings of the Taoists and the Ayurvedics to reveal the universality of categorizing the bits and pieces of the universe along elemental lines.

We'll pick up the story in ancient Greece, at the point in history when Earth, Air, Fire, and Water are transformed into the Four Elements—a moniker given to them by the seminal philosopher Plato. In this tale, these previously disparate forces are inadvertently, and irrevocably, banded together by a bunch of Greek geeks attempting to find the Building Blocks of Everything. Previously, the elements were thought of as powers of nature and were often personified as gods and goddesses. But, in their own way, the Greeks were developing a theory similar to the modern theory of the atom. They were looking for the component pieces that make up the universe, and Earth, Air, Fire, and Water found themselves at the center of the drama.

After gaining an understanding of how the Four Elements achieved their superpower status, we'll segue into learning a smidge about alchemy. Alchemy is a science that worked with the Four Elements. To bring it back to the kitchen: the four elements are the various ingredients you need to make a loaf of bread, and the alchemical process is the recipe that turns those ingredients into something tasty.

Note: This course is a prerequisite for Harnessing the Celestial Tides. Not only have the elements been used to understand life on Earth, they have also been used to explain the Night sky.

And another note: In a last-minute plot twist, we'll be starting at the end instead of the beginning.

Topics covered include:

LESSON 11:	The Modern Elements
LESSON 1:	Developing a Theory of Everything
LESSON 2:	Getting Grounded in the Elements
LESSON 3:	Earth
LESSON 4:	Water
LESSON 5:	Air
LESSON 6:	Fire
LESSON 7:	From Elements to . . . Everything!
LESSON 8:	The Invention of Alchemy
LESSON 9:	The Elements, Alchemy, and You
LESSON 10:	Simultaneous Discovery

While I normally suggest one lesson per Night, you might find yourself gaining speed as you move through lessons 2–6. To make acceleration easier through these lessons, you'll notice they don't have any homework.

After the elemental straightaway, you'll want to slow back down to navigate the curves in lessons 7–10. Be sure to pause for homework, which is still due to your journal 72 hours after the lesson is complete.

You might find yourself getting creative with how you mark a lesson as finished: perhaps an elemental glyph to match your mood?

Here they are in all their triangular glory:

FIRE

AIR

WATER

EARTH

Lesson 11:

THE MODERN ELEMENTS

Let's begin at the end, shall we? Because sometimes it's fun to eat dessert first.

On February 17, 1869, Dmitri Ivanovich Mendeleev, a Russian professor of chemistry, completed a periodic chart of the known elements.

Earth, Air, Fire, and Water, the four classic elements, were not on the chart.

This was no surprise to chemists. The classic four had long been supplanted. And it wasn't just Mendeleev who thought so. Others had been working toward the same end for the hundred years prior to Mendeleev's "discovery." But Mendeleev's chart brought a previously unshown order to the ongoing enterprise of redefining the basic elements of the universe.

One of the fabulous features of Mendeleev's periodic table was that, in addition to the 63 known elements arranged according to increasing atomic weight, his organizing structure included not only space for but a prediction of the atomic weight of elements he believed would be discovered in the future.

(Who said that scientists can't practice divination, Firefly?)

At the time that Mendeleev developed his periodic table, the smallest possible division of matter was thought to be the atom.

Since then, the periodic table has grown to 112 known elements. (Not one of which is Earth, Air, Water, or Fire. Yes, I'm being repetitive, but I really want to make sure this incredible change in the molecular structure of the entire universe is sinking in.) The atom is now thought to be made up of protons, neutrons, and electrons. And protons and neutrons are made up of even smaller particles called quarks.

As of this moment, quarks are the smallest known particle, the most infinitesimal building block, and the tiniest division of matter.

(Although scientists are theorizing that there may be something tinier—they're calling it a *leptoquark*. Stay tuned!)

Why am I telling you this, Firefly?

First, to show you that intellectual history is always evolving. It's an expansive, daytime discipline that is constantly reaching and growing. It's the ultimate yang endeavor. Because of this perpetual movement and growth, there is no final answer, only the answer *for now* . . . which leads to the next question . . . and the next answer.

But these daylight discoveries are not the only truths. The Night has its own logic. Even as science advances, there is something in our Night-nature that still resonates strongly with the original four elements of Earth, Air, Water, and Fire. I've never had an encounter with strontium or neodymium (Sr and Nd on the periodic table) in the collective unconscious. And I've yet to run into a witch who calls in the powers of protons, electrons, neutrons, and quarks when casting a spell circle.

Our day-brains now know that Earth, Air, Water, and Fire are not the primary building blocks of the universe. Instead we have atoms and their component parts. And yet our Night-brains hardly seem to notice this newish knowledge: our romance with the four elements remains. Over their multitudinous centuries of existence in our consciousness, they've carved out a place for themselves in the C.U.

Although Earth, Air, Fire, and Water are iconic, we've lost some of their history, which means we no longer fully experience the layered symbolism and meanings of these elements, even though they are often used in magic and ritual. What's more, many mystics are simply following a recipe—two parts Earth, three parts Water, double-double toil and trouble—and no longer have a basic understanding of why the recipe works. (If you're a kitchen witch and want to dive into the whys of a recipe, I highly recommend *Salt, Fat, Acid, Heat* by Samin Nosrat. I'll make a note in the Additional Resources at the end of the course for you, Firefly.)

The truth is, when you lack a clear understanding of the basics, all you can do is follow a recipe. But if you want to riff and improvise, if you want to create never-dreamed-of concoctions and delicious derivations on the usual themes, you need to understand your ingredients. Anyone can make a pizza, Firefly, but only someone who understands both cheese—the various lactic bacteria used to make its cultures—and dough—the lengths of rest-time the yeast needs to create the perfect blend of fluffy and crisp—only that well-versed person can create a truly celestial pie.

It's the same with magic. If you want to follow recipes, you don't need this course. But if you want to become an alchemist, then you need to develop a mastery of the ingredients you're working with.

So, without further ado, I bring you the evolution of the Original Building Blocks of the Universe.

Homework: Symbolism Soup

As you continue on with this course, pay attention to and look for how the history of the elements has created the rich and layered texture of their symbolism. Just like a soup is better on the second day and whiskey mellows and deepens with age, the elements have become multidimensional on their travel through the ages.

For the duration of this coursework, keep notes in your journal on the four elements. Track which elements appear in your Night-life and in what form. Are you dreaming of Fire? Meditating with Water? Suddenly aware of all the Earth that surrounds you in your home?

Take notes so you can track how the elements are tracking you!

DEVELOPING A THEORY OF EVERYTHING

Once humans grappled their way high enough up Maslow's hierarchy to be able to contemplate life beyond the next meal, they started asking themselves the questions that still haunt us today: *What are we? Why are we? What is everything around us made of and made for?* And the natural corollary: *if we figure all this stuff out, will our lives feel rich and meaningful?*

This ongoing attempt to understand both human nature and the composition of the universe has kept philosophers and scientists busy for eons.

(And we still don't have *the* answer, Firefly. Anyone who tells you we do is running a cult or trying to sell you something.

Oh?! You thought you were going to find THE ANSWER here? At the Night School?

Don't despair. While we're fresh out of answers, what we do have is an abundance of beautiful questions. And questions are so much better than answers.

Answers are *the end.* Questions are the beginning. Questions are keys. Keys open doors. Doors are thresholds—liminal space—leading to somewhere else . . .

When you step through a doorway, anything is possible . . . And that's what we focus on at the Night School. Leave the absolutes to the lawyers.)

As I was saying before I sidetracked myself:

This ongoing attempt to understand both human nature and the composition of the universe has kept philosophers and scientists busy for eons.

For the early part of those eons, philosophers tried to find the one, ultimate building block that they could be assured made up all things. Atom, anyone?

But, alas, atomdom was still millennia away. So when finding one irreducible building block didn't work out, Empedocles of Acragas (c. 495–

c. 435 BCE) proposed that there were four: Earth, Air, Water, and Fire. This was taken up, discussed, dissected, and satirized.

But through it all, the idea of four elements stuck . . . and that influenced everything that came after.

It's easy to look at the concept of the four elements as simply a hot trend in the Hellenistic world. But consider a few things:

* As hard as it is to believe, given the lack of engines and airplanes, people traveled quite a bit back before the common era. They traded all sorts of things including, and maybe most importantly, ideas. And these ancient intellectuals? They were the original foreign exchange students. For example, Aristotle spent over a decade in Alexandria. (That's in Egypt, Firefly. Both Africa and Asia claim a piece of Egypt, so it's confusing to say exactly which continent's learning the teachings of Alexandria represent.)

* There's a concept in intellectual history called *multiple discovery* or *simultaneous invention*. The basic idea is that when the cultural conditions are ripe, the next phase of thought will, synchronistically, form in multiple people's heads. We have a whole lesson on this later in the course.

So while we happen to be tracking the four elements from the vantage point of ancient Greece, you could also track their development in ancient India, Tibet, or China.

(Why Greece, you may wonder? That's a personal proclivity, Firefly. I've actually stood in the ruins of the Temple of Apollo at Delphi, but have yet to make it to India, Tibet, or China—or Alexandria for that matter! But that shouldn't stop you from pulling on the threads that capture *your* imagination to see where they take you. I have a theory that all the rabbit holes lead to the same burrow, but I have yet to prove it!)

Homework: Take a Trip

Do a little world tour by research, Firefly, and catalog how many cultures around the globe have a concept similar to the idea of the four elements. See if you can date the origin of these thought patterns in various cultures. How many cultures were involved in an almost simultaneous discovery of similar elemental principles?

Once you have that information, craft an essay that contemplates the effect of the collective unconscious in our global intellectual history.

OR

Ponder the role of Night-thoughts on our daytime discoveries.

Extra Credit: Explore the History of the Atom

While we usually think of the atom as a modern concept, it was first conceived at a surprisingly early point in history. Do a little research so you can be surprised for yourself!

Research hint: *Democritus.*

Lesson 2:

GETTING GROUNDED IN THE ELEMENTS

Take a look at the room where you're reading tonight. Notice the candles you've lit to study by (Fire for the flames, Earth for the candle, and Air to keep the flame ignited), the cup of tea waiting patiently in its mug (Earth and Water), and the stars sparkling beyond your window (that's a lovely mélange of Earth and Water for the window glass and Fire for the stars, unless you're feeling Aristotelian and want to contemplate the question of whether or not the stars fall into the divine realm of Aether).

As you look around and realize your space is chock-full of elements, you can begin to understand why, until the discoveries made by modern physics and biology, the four elements were thought to be the foundational materials of the universe. As we've established, metaphorically, they still are.

Because the four elements are indelibly written into our languages and cultures, you probably don't need me to spell them out. Still, it's worth a quick run-through so you can be sure to recognize them roaming free— or in your tarot deck or astrology chart where they play a starring role. Be sure to read the following descriptions with your Night-goggles firmly in place so you can get a *feel* for each element.

Remember that for our purposes here, the four elements are symbols and glyphs that may help you read the patterns you're seeing in the world around you. Understanding their multilayered usage, which has in turn built up multilayered symbolism, will help you interpret these building blocks when you run into them in a dream or divination. Studying the elements both as actual manifestations and as metaphor will take you deeper into the mysterious patterns of the Night that humans have been tracking for millennia.

And don't forget: you can return to this place of noticing the elemental world around you if the lessons become too ethereal and you begin to get lost in the thought forms. Physical reality is immensely grounding, so use your senses and tune in to the elements as an antidote to the brain vaporization caused by large doses of theory.

We'll move through each of the elements as a stand-alone lesson. There won't be homework (starting now), so you can fast-track it if you want and arrive at the later lessons where we see how the elements play together!

P.S. For the next four lessons, note that you're looking at a modern interpretation of the elements. We'll get to their ancient origins in a bit!

Lesson 3:

EARTH

Your derriere is most likely resting on something made from the element of Earth. (This gets tricky if you're in bed, Firefly. Then the possibilities expand: a regular mattress is Earth, an air mattress is self-explanatory, and having a waterbed is very 1970s of you, as well as being elementally Watery. If you're doing dream work, the composition of your mattress could be a defining influence: a nocturnal fantasy gala where the guests show up in bell-bottoms and the band plays "Staying Alive" would have different connotations if you were floating on a waterbed instead of sleeping on your run-of-the-mill, Earth-based, mattress material.)

Earth is stabilizing, making it a fine element for mattresses and other furniture. Material things—like humans, chairs, and carrots—are made of Earth and will eventually return to Earth. This is not mere metaphor (as if metaphor were ever mere!). Microbes in the soil break down and compost natural materials. The breakdown of these materials allows them to be reused, becoming building blocks for something new. It's like breaking apart a Lego set you had previously used to build a castle and reusing all the pieces to make a bulldozer. Of course, Legos, like many other things we humans have made, are plastic. Plastic befuddles the little microbes in the soil, and they can't break it down. (Plastic, ironically, is the last in a chain of events that started with microbes breaking down ancient Earth-stuff and turning it into petroleum. Humans then get a hold of the petroleum and turn it into plastics, which incidentally totally confound the microbes. Who said there's no such thing as cosmic double jeopardy, Firefly?)

Something almost as crazy as our human need to foil the soil microbes is the way the Earth outside of us speaks to the Earth within us. Science is getting in on a secret that gardeners have known for a long time: digging in the dirt might just make you happier. Turns out there's a soil microbe called *Mycobacterium vaccae* that helps your body build serotonin levels. Serotonin is your body's way of combating stress and depression. Gardeners get a dose of *Mycobacterium vaccae* through topical contact with the soil, as well as by inhaling microscopic particles kicked up by digging. Earth communing with Earth for the greater good.

> In the tarot deck Earth aligns with pentacles.
>
> In astrology it is represented by Taurus, Virgo, and Capricorn.
>
> Your main takeaways on the Earth element:
>
> · Both actually and metaphorically, it's about structure and the ability to compost.
>
> · Earth returns to Earth in the end. (Keep this principle in mind, Firefly: it will become important when we discuss alchemy.)

Lesson 4:

WATER

At its most basic level, Water is the stuff in the glass or mug you're drinking from. It doesn't matter what kind of liquid is in the cup: if it's a liquid, it falls under the Water element. Remember, none of this is written in stone (which, by the way, would be the Earth element). Some philosophers say that the only 100-percent-pure elements are conceptual elements; that once they materialize and have form, they're all hybrids and mutts. So, for instance, gasoline would be a blend of Earth and Water, because, even though it's liquid (Water), it's made from fossils (Earth). Or you could get fancy, call it Liquid Earth, trademark it, and start a whole other discussion . . .

And this would be a perfectly legitimate and Watery tangent, because Water is *mutable*: it can move from solid (ice) to liquid (water) to air (vapor). So Water is liquid—except when it's not. Because of this inherent mutability, water represents that which is mutable within us—our emotions (which gives you a clue about the healthiest emotional state, Firefly: both standing water and stuck emotions get stinky).

Water is associated with cleansing. Remember this when you're looking at mythology. The River Styx in Greek mythology is, for instance, the demarcation between the underworld and the everyday world we inhabit. But to see it only as a boundary is to forget your Night-goggles. When you remember that the Styx is a *river*, and therefore ruled by the Water element, you can bring the concept of cleansing into your symbolic analysis. This, in turn, helps you understand that the Styx washes away the residue of life to prepare you for what's next. (If you're an ancient Greek, this is thankfully not hellfire and damnation. You can begin to see why I've become so enchanted with their philosophies, Firefly.)

In the tarot deck Water aligns with cups.

In astrology it is represented by Cancer, Scorpio, Pisces.

Your main takeaways on the Water element are:

- Water is mutable and can change forms.
- Keywords for this element are *cleanse* and *flow*.

Lesson 5:

AIR

Air is the catalyst of the four element system and so represents change. Air's turnabouts can be quick, often happening at the speed of thought (as in: *I changed my mind! I don't want sushi for that midnight snack; I think I'd prefer pie. . .*).

Air can seem as conceptual as the quark, but it's fairly easy to attune to its movement once you know where to look. Start with your own breath—inhale, exhale. That's Air. If you listen, you can hear it in the quiet whoosh of the heated or air-conditioned drafts passing through the vents, or in the wind rustling the Night branches. Air carries scent and sound at varying rates, traversing and distorting distances in much the same way our minds can warp time and space.

So metaphorically, Air reflects the gymnastics the brain performs as it does its light-speed thinkings. Because we understand Air best when it is in motion, it metaphorically aligns with movement and change—thus the expression "the winds of change." Using the rhythm of your breath or the vibrations of a drum to transport yourself to the collective unconscious, Air becomes a vehicle you can drive toward a place within yourself, a place where you can experience a mental shift—a change in consciousness.

The ancient Greeks differentiated two types of air: *aer* meant the changeable lower atmosphere below the clouds, while *aether* meant the atmosphere above the clouds, which was thought to be constant and unchanging. Aristotle separated aether (or, in more modern terms, ether) from the regular air you and I breathe. Aether for Aristotle was a divine element that was the fundamental building block of the heavens.

While I have no daylight evidence of this, Firefly, I suspect that Aristotle debated the elements with an Ayurvedic practitioner from the Hindu school of thought. That lineage adds ether to the original four elements, and it makes Night-sense that exposure to this tradition of inquiry would have influenced Aristotle's thinking.

More than any other element, Air is life—which, really, is the ultimate catalyst. You can live without Water for about three days. You can go without food (which would be the Earth element) for more than eight. Death by hypothermia (not enough heat, or, in elemental terms the lack of the Fire element) takes around 15 minutes. But you can only go without air for 5 to 10 minutes before suffering irrevocable brain death. Without external Air, your internal Air (that's your thinking) is extinguished.

In the tarot deck Air aligns with Swords.

In astrology it is represented by Gemini, Libra, Aquarius.

Your main takeaways:

- Air represents a catalyst and, as such, signifies change, as well as the intellect.
- The vibrations of Air can help you achieve altered states of consciousness.

Extra Credit

Wanna play hooky?

Put down your book and watch the movie *Chocolat*. Keep an eye out for the Air element in action!

I know I said no homework, Firefly, so consider this a super-fun extra credit.

Lesson 6:

FIRE

Fire is the trickster of the elements. Just ask anyone who has been in love. With a little combustion, you can quickly get a first flame. But going from first flame to a sustained Fire is an art that humans are still learning.

Fire was the one element that didn't come right to our hand. The earliest humanoid gasped in a first breath of Air, sat on the Earth to rest, and lay on the banks of a river to sip from the flowing Water. But Fire was elusive: it radiated down from the sun and flashed across the dark blanket of sky as lightning and shooting stars. It was a thing of the heavens, which occasionally came to the ground only to wreak havoc. And, like all things divine, humans craved it.

Once we had it, Fire changed everything.

So how did people achieve mastery of this godlike element?

Stories vary—and all we have is stories, Firefly: the taming of Fire took place long before there was written record. In fact, the first evidence of Fire, based on identifying and dating charcoal residue, took place in what geologists call *deep time*—the stretch of the Earth's history before Homo sapiens inhabited it. The Greeks credit the titan Prometheus with stealing it from the gods, the Tagish peoples of Canada tell the tale of Crow bringing Fire, and in Polynesian mythology, it was stolen from the Fire goddess Mahuika. In all these stories, Fire is brought down from the celestial realm of the sky.

And, most likely, that's what actually happened: a lightning strike caused a small fire, which our early ancestors captured and nurtured, carrying it from campfire to campfire, revering it for the warmth it provided. In a literal flash, Fire-keeping became the most important position in any hunter/gatherer group.

Fire provided more than a warm place to sleep protected from other animals (who still saw Fire and thought *RUN!*): Fire gave these early humanoids a place to roast marshmallows and toast s'mores. Since it's well known that the nutritional value of marshmallows and graham crackers can only be unlocked when cooked, mastering the Fire element for cooking meant that food suddenly had a higher nutritional value. (Kidding aside, Firefly, when you cook food, you begin to break down the fibers and proteins, essentially predigesting it, so that by the time you put the food inside your stomach, there's less work to do in order to assimilate the nutritional components.) A study out of the Institute of Biomedical Sciences at the Federal University of Rio de Janeiro in Brazil was able to match the timelines for cooking food with the relative brain size of our ancestor, *Homo erectus*. The gradual introduction of fire-cooked food ran parallel with a doubling in their brain size, which took place over the course of some 600,000 years.

You can see from Fire's prehistoric beginnings why it became the element associated with warmth and passion. And these earliest Fire users had to be abundantly creative to move from barbecue to *brûlée*. Don't forget, the words for *cook* and *magic* were the same in Ancient Greek. That makes more sense now, doesn't it, Firefly? The cook was the magician who doubled our brain capacity, thus creating mental space to dream up roller derby, roadsters, and rock and roll.

Over time, people discovered that Fire had uses beyond warming food and fingers. Fire's ability to heat metal took us from the Stone Age to the Bronze Age. The expression "burning off the dross" comes from metalwork, where heat is applied to burn off impurities. This explains why alchemically, purification is Fire's transformation. You can see this at play in your own kitchen: when you make a broth, a sludgy film forms as the liquid heats. These impurities can be skimmed off and fed to the dogs (who are great helpers in dealing with impurities of all sorts).

Fire has always managed to be both elusive, necessary, and, on occasion, overwhelming. Keep these descriptors in mind in the next lesson when we explore alchemical transformation.

A final thing to remember: Fire can't ignite without Air. (You can't light a match in a vacuum, Firefly. It's most frustrating.)

Note: If you're noticing that the job descriptions of the elements sometimes overlap—especially if we're comparing alchemical elements to how the elements are used by the modern mystic—you would be right! But with your Night-goggles firmly in place, you'll see that Fire's role as the alchemical purifier doesn't prohibit Water from also taking up those duties in your own practices.

In the tarot deck Fire aligns with wands.

In astrology it is represented by Aries, Leo, Sagittarius.

The takeaways for the Fire element:

· Fire is symbolic of passion and creativity.

· This element is a transformer and purifier, as well as the trickster of the elements. (When you read stories of how humans got Fire, keep an eye out for trickster animals like coyote and raven to somehow be involved!)

Lesson 7:

FROM ELEMENTS TO . . . EVERYTHING!

How, you might be wondering, did we go from a theory in which the four elements acted as building blocks and essentially the atoms of their day to the four elements influencing everything from tarot and astrology, to medicine, to color theory and interior design? We don't talk about whether a blue sofa enhances a quark's quarkiness but, in both the Chinese system of feng shui and the Indian Vastu Shastra, the color, and placement, of your couch is used to enhance the elemental balance of your home.

How did the concept of the four elements become entwined with so many human systems?

To understand this leap, Firefly, you have to return to the fundamental principles we discussed in your first Night School course, Midnight Foundations. In the ancient world—and not just the Greek one—the fundamental precept *as above, so below* was de rigueur. Equally as important was the concept of balancing dualities—this is what the yin/yang circle symbolizes.

So once the elements were decided upon, people not only looked for them everywhere and in everything (because the micro reflects the macro and vice versa), they also considered it their sacred duty to help maintain the balance of the universe by doing their fair share to keep the elements in equilibrium. In the same way you make sure you're eating from a variety of food groups, ancient folks made sure their lives were made up of a balanced blend of elements. Why did they do this? Because they believed that this balance contributed to humanity's harmony with the divine, as well as to their personal health and well-being.

While this explains *why* the four elements appeared in everything from medicine to fashion (yes, in the Ayurvedic system, you wear certain colors to help keep your internal elements in balance), it still doesn't explain *how* this happened.

The most important thing to understand, Firefly, is that at this point in history day-brain and Night-brain were both seen as equally valuable (that's the balance principle in action!). And, perhaps because of this, the various disciplines of academia were seen, not as separate, but as interconnected. Aristotle and Co. would be befuddled by modern compartmentalized thinking. Today a discovery in religious studies is rarely read by biology majors and, even more surprising, a revelation in chemistry might never make its way into the minds of those studying to be doctors. But in Aristotle's day, great thinkers thought together, mind-melding on a vast array of topics.

Want to have a little fun, Firefly? Let's join Aristotle and Co. in the C.U. to see how this whole four elements thing went down (at least for them—remember, there is a wide world out there, and similar thoughts were being thunk by brilliant people in many cultures).

Imagine that you've slipped into a booth at the C.U. Cafe, where a rollicking debate is well underway about the nature of the four, or maybe five, elements. *How can this elemental theory be used in daily life?* Aristotle wonders. *How does it explain how a flower grows or why a person gets ill?*

Aristotle grabs a napkin and gestures for your pen, which you dutifully hand over. On the napkin he writes:

Fire–Water

Earth–Air

He pauses. Is Air the same as Sky? He shakes his head noncommittally and continues jotting.

Aether?

Meanwhile Galen (who in real time could never hang out with Aristotle and Co. but is enjoying this perk of being in the C.U.) is doodling on his own napkin, pairing the elements with both the seasons of the year and of people's lives:

Air–Spring–Infancy

Fire–Summer–Youth

Earth–Autumn–Adulthood

Water–Winter–Old Age

(If you've studied Wicca or modern witchcraft, Firefly, you might be thinking I just made an error. But I didn't. Ideas change over time, which is a fabulous reason not to get too fixed in your thinking and also not to believe everything you read.)

Napkins are flying. Ideas are being exchanged.

Aristotle is onto something with his lists, something that would drive this four element theory from the womb of the Night and into the bright light of day, where it would impact the arts and sciences for a thousand years to come.

Eventually, Aristotle produces this:

Hippocrates, the father of modern medicine, looks over his shoulder and says, *I think I can work with that!* He goes on to create a whole new concept of disease theory.

(Why, you might be wondering, did Aristotle's vision of the four elements become the dominant way of thinking when there were lots of other philosophers working on the same issue? Aristotle was the influencer of his day, Firefly. Whatever he posted got shared and re-shared, making it easier to accept his thoughts as truth.)

Homework: You and the Elements

Before you begin your homework, Firefly, walk yourself back out of the C.U. (Close the door behind you, please.) Shake off the sense of otherness and make yourself a cup of tea. When you're ready, do a little journaling.

Think about how you conceptualize the four elements. Do they have mystical meaning for you? Do you work with them in your Night-life? What schools of thought have influenced how you perceive the elements? Are you limiting their (and, therefore, your) potential by viewing them only through a specific lens? Finally, what do you think of the idea of including a fifth element—ether, space, or the void—into the League of Elements? What would the properties of this fifth element be?

Lesson 8:

THE INVENTION OF ALCHEMY

As we move forward in time, we find ourselves in the seventh century. Things were a bit shaky as the Roman Empire had dissolved, and scholarship was on the wane. But the Arabs began an intellectual revival. Greek books were translated into Arabic, which is how the Aristotelian theory of the four elemental qualities (the *hot, cold, dry, wet* that he doodled on a napkin in the C.U.) became the base upon which alchemy was built.

While in our current jargon we call any type of pre–scientific trans-formational work "alchemy," the word is actually of Arabic etymology. *Al-kimiya,* in its original meaning, is not merely a loose collection of pre-science, but instead the practical and theoretical knowledge needed to transmute base metals into noble ones. (This is the whole "lead into gold" thing, Firefly.) The Arabic alchemists based their theories on the elemental philosophies of the Greeks, as well as philosophies from China and India. These were braided together with the practical knowledge and trade secrets of the ancient metallurgists, dyers, and embalmers of ancient Egypt and Persia. This amalgam of knowledge was called *al-kimiya.* Alchemy.

The early Arabic alchemists were experimenters. They excelled at tak-ing theory and turning it into practice. This is important to remember, because Aristotle wasn't a laboratory kind of guy—he was a theorist. His theories, while a wonderful base from which the Arabic alchemists could begin their experiments, were untested in the material realm. The experi-ments the alchemists performed focused on replicating natural processes.

Why? Because a lot of the stuff that was considered valuable—then and now—was hard to find and hard to mine. Wouldn't it be great if you could make your own gold, for instance?

It's easy, from our modern perches, to make fun of the alchemists for trying to turn lead into gold. But we owe a great debt to the Arabic alchemists, both from a scientific and a mystical aspect (as you'll see in the next lesson).

Let's take a quick tour of the steps involved in this daylight form of alchemy so we can see if it expands our understanding of the four ele-ments and their Nighttime applications.

The alchemist takes raw material—*prima materia*—which is a solid, and through a series of transformations, inspired and often mediated by the four elements, encourages it to change form.

(You can return to the lesson *Alchemy and Laundry Have a Lot in Common* from Midnight Foundations to be reminded of some of these transformational processes, Firefly.)

The alchemist's "first matter" is the Earth element. It's a solid and might seem unchangeable.

But through alchemy it is transformed into a liquid, which is the Water element.

Then it's transformed from liquid into gas, which is the Air element.

Then it's transformed from gas into plasma, which is the Fire element.

And finally the material returns to solid (Earth), thus beginning the cycle again.

Is this just a thought exercise? you might be wondering. *Why the heck would anyone want to do this?*

When we ground this in some kitchen reality, Firefly, I think I can convince you that the alchemical cycle can create something delicious!

Let's say you're going to make Bananas Foster, a gooey, caramelized topping which is delicious on vanilla ice cream. (Even if you don't like bananas, Firefly, please stay with the class and envision yourself walking through these alchemical transformations.) First you pull out a stick of butter. It's a solid (Earth), but you apply heat and melt it into a liquid (Water). You then add sugar and cinnamon. When it's bubbly, you add the bananas. Meanwhile, you heat some rum to just below boiling. This creates evaporation, which is the Air element at play. And now, for the final act, you light a long kitchen match, set the rum on Fire, and combine the still flaming liquid back with those earthy bananas and stir.

(For goodness' sake, Firefly, do not try this with a typical short match or a lighter because you *will* burn your fingers. But if you decide to play with Fire, despite my warning—because someone always does—run your singed fingertips under cold Water, then apply a generous amount of *Lavandula angustifolia* essential oil. Then more Water, then more lavender oil, until the burning subsides. Pure lavender essential oil is an absolute necessity in the alchemical kitchen.)

Homework: Flambé, Eat, and Ponder

Tonight's homework is your Alchemy Lab. Go make Bananas Foster!

You'll need:

6 tablespoons butter

½ cup brown sugar, firmly packed

½ teaspoon ground cinnamon

4 bananas, halved lengthwise

¾ cup rum

Melt the butter until it's a liquid. Add sugar and cinnamon. Cook over medium heat until it's bubbly, then add the bananas; heat for 3–4 minutes, basting the bananas constantly with the syrup.

Now is when we add the fire: first pour the rum in a small, long-handled pan and heat just until it's warm. Then ignite the rum with a long match and carefully pour the flaming alcohol over the bananas, making sure the banana pan is away from the heat source of your stove.

Baste bananas with sauce until flames die down.

Serve immediately over ice cream or pancakes or peanut butter brownies.

While you're enjoying your dessert, I have a fun sidenote for you:

From its inception, alchemy was a secretive art. In the very beginning—before the word *alchemy* even existed—practitioners sought to keep their experiments under wraps because this type of chemistry created a bridge from the world of mundane matter into the realms of the divine. Ancient Egyptian "alchemy" held the secrets of embalming, so the dead could pass into the afterlife with their bodies intact. This tradition also passed on the mysteries of crafting with glass and metal, an art form that, at the time, was considered god-touched.

By the Middle Ages, the focus of alchemy was on metallurgy and chemistry. It had moved from a practice that bridged the worlds of day and Night into a more purely daytime way of thinking.

The modern mind has decided that medieval alchemy held its secrets close because practitioners knew the magic of transmuting lead into gold or had found the elixir of eternal life. But, most likely, it was a combination of not wanting the uninitiated (as in people who don't know what the heck they're doing) to play with things that go boom, keeping trade secrets (in the same way an inventor would get a patent today), and being cagey with the Christian church, which was less than thrilled that humans were messing around with the stuff of creation. So, for centuries, alchemy books were purposefully obtuse, requiring the reader to learn a language of symbolism before interpreting them.

All this changed in the 16th century, when a new genre was created: *the book of secrets*. These books contained straightforward alchemical recipes that could be used in everyday life—recipes for everything from dyeing cloth to preserving foods to making cosmetics—and they quickly became immensely popular.

The *Secrets* of Isabella Cortese was published in Venice in 1561. (Look: a woman's name! Finally: a welcome change to our cast of characters!) The *Secrets* was translated into German for two editions and reprinted in Italy 15 times.

I couldn't resist that little side trip to introduce you to Isabella. Plus Venice is always worth a visit, especially if we're talking alchemy: it was the home of the infamous alchemist Bragadini, who claimed to have discovered the secret of turning lead into gold. Interestingly, he passed many tests of his ability to produce bullion, but he never seemed to be able to scale up the operation to the satisfaction of his benefactors and was eventually beheaded.

Lesson 9:

THE ELEMENTS, ALCHEMY, AND YOU

When you made your Bananas Foster, Firefly, you brought your original bananas through a full alchemical cycle—they started as prima materia, were transformed by Water, Air, and Fire respectively, and, when you were done with the recipe, they had returned back to a solid (a gooey solid, but a representation of the Earth element nonetheless). Their dance through the alchemical cycle had changed a previously breakfast-worthy banana into a fitting dessert.

Huh, an alchemist pondered, watching these transformations. *Can we do the same thing for the human psyche? Take a person we'd normally share a quick breakfast with and turn them into a person who we want to canoodle with all the way through dinner's dessert?*

If you've encountered alchemy as a psychological art, you might have attributed this thought to our friend Carl Jung. And while Carl did revive the concept of psychological alchemy in the 20th century, the origin of the concept should probably be attributed to Muhammad ibn Umail al-Tamimi, an alchemist from the 10th century. I'd love to tell you where he was from, Firefly, but the record is a bit shaky: maybe Andalusia, maybe Egypt. Either way, Muhammad ibn Umail al-Tamimi was an Islamic mystic and symbolic alchemist. Physical alchemy, to him, was a Trojan horse. Instead he read the symbols and transformations of alchemy as a metaphor for transmuting the (metaphoric) lead within oneself to (metaphoric) gold.

This was a new way of approaching alchemy . . . or was it?

From deep time forward, alchemy was an art of the Night, acting as a bridge into the realms of death and the divine. Even before the four elements were named as the Building Blocks of All Things, they were used in this ancient form of alchemy. At that point, the elements were viewed as forces of nature or gods and goddesses. (Look up "Wind God" or "Sun Goddesses" and you'll find long lists from across the globe.)

Over the centuries, alchemy became a material art, more about science and craft than the unseen worlds of the Night. But then we see Muhammad ibn Umail al-Tamimi beginning the reclamation, taking back the four elements and claiming an alchemy for the psyche.

Realizing that the human spirit can transform is a *re-newed* thought. In our brief trip down memory lane, we've watched alchemy itself undergo the process of transforming from one thing to the next, and then returning to the solid state of Earth, but in an enhanced way. It's kind of like climbing a spiral staircase, Firefly: you go round in a circle and yet you are never in the same place twice. (Sound familiar from your foundational principles?)

So the thing-that-was-later-called-alchemy began with the gods and with myth. It began in the realm of the Night. Then it became an art that bridged day and Night, helping usher the dead into the spirit world. Through the early part of the Middle Ages, alchemy was mainly a part of the daylight world: it was a way of rationally manipulating physical material. (No, it does not seem rational by today's scientific standards, but it was rational when placed in historical context. And while the secrecy around alchemy created an air of mystery, let's not confuse top-secret with mystical.)

Muhammad ibn Umail al-Tamimi completed the circle when he imagined an alchemy of the spirit. In some ways this new alchemy recalls Aristotle's theory of the elements as foundational building blocks *which can only exist in the conceptual realm*. But more importantly, it brings us full circle up the spiral staircase: when alchemy and the elements were new, they were the domain of the gods and goddesses—used to make both welcome and unwelcome changes in human lives by blowing in good fortune or raining down flames. But through a millennia's long transformational process, alchemy has become a technique through which we can take control of our own lives, using the building blocks of all things to remake ourselves, giving us, in that moment of creativity, access to something greater than our present moment.

So, in this move from working with matter to working with spirit, the Four Elements took another step toward becoming a part of a Theory of All Things. But perhaps more importantly for our purposes, Firefly, when alchemy became not just a physical science but a spiritual one as well, when the four elements began to be used as part of a psychological rubric for personal transformation, elemental alchemy became an art of the Night. Our Night-selves can work with not only the alchemical process itself (see page 36) but also the symbolism of the Four Elements.

How exactly does all this work, you might wonder?

Your homework will help you to figure it out!

Homework: Use the Four Elements
for Personal Transformation

Let's imagine, Firefly, that there is something you want to change about yourself. (I know you're pretty spectacular just as you are, but imagine the wondrousness you could achieve if you conquered your fear of heights or resolved your relationship with your brother.)

How might you go about using the alchemy of the four elements—either metaphorically or materially—to create a change in your own life? Remember alchemy is concerned with change and transformation. So another way to say this would be, how can you create an alchemical transmutation in your own life using the four elements and alchemical principles?

Your thought process might look something like this:

I've been so angry at (insert the name of the person you're holding a grudge against) for a long time. When I think of this person, my

heart feels like a stone. Stone is Earth. Things grow in Earth and plantings break up compacted soil allowing Air and Water to come through. Maybe I can imagine planting a rosebush in the hurt place in my heart and tending to it every day. Perhaps this would let my emotions (Water) flow and allow new thoughts (Air) to influence my feelings.

I know this exercise might sound absolutely intimidating. Don't panic! Remember, every step of the elemental and alchemical process has been discussed and debated for eons, which means there isn't a right answer. This is a creative exercise, not a quiz. So put on your Night-goggles, relax, and contemplate the wind blowing your worries away or writing all your angst on slips of paper that you feed to your wood-burning stove. Imagine arming your dream self with a magical elixir to ease a reconciliation and sprinkling that elixir on the left toe of a person who has hurt you when you happen to meet their spirit-self in the C.U. Cafe.

Be creative, be outrageous, and most of all believe that a change you create in the Night can resonate and affect your day-life.

(Yes, this imagining is the beginning step to creating a ritual. How astute of you to notice!)

Lesson 10:

SIMULTANEOUS DISCOVERY

While the Greeks and the Arabs were moving from elements to alchemy, and from Night to day and back again, so were other cultures around the globe. None of these discoveries were happening in a vacuum, Firefly: the Greeks and Arabs were being educated and influenced by the cultures around them and vice versa.

Let's take a quick peek at ideas about the elements that influenced thinking about them both then and now. We'll look through the lens of healing because it allows us to compare bananas with bananas. Let's start in Greece and then check out near simultaneous happenings in India and China.

Greece

The Hippocratic system, known as the humoral system, was built on the idea of assigning the elements the characteristics hot, cold, wet, and dry. (This is where the concept of "having a cold" comes from, Firefly.) In the humoral system you became unwell when the elements within you were out of balance.

India

While I have no direct evidence of this, Firefly, I suspect Hippocrates's ideas were likely influenced by Ayurvedic medicine which was, in another act of simultaneous discovery, being documented in India around the time Hippocrates was getting the humoral system off the ground. Note that I say *being documented*, not *being discovered*. It's hard to pin down a precise beginning for Ayurvedic medicine, because for centuries it was handed down as an oral tradition. It is undoubtably among the oldest medicines, but that doesn't tell us when the concept of the elements was integrated into its workings. What we can say for certain is that in the period of time during which Hippocrates was noodling over the necessaries of using Earth, Air, Water, and Fire as a basis for balancing the human body, Ayurvedic medical philosophies began to appear in writing—making them accessible for someone like, say, Hippocrates.

The Ayurvedic system goes in for the full five elements of Earth, Air, Fire, Water, and Ether, which then combine in various ways to create three basic constitutional types or *doshas*:

* Vata people are a combination of Ether and Air.

* Pitta people are a combination of Fire and Water.

* Kapha people are a combination of Water and Earth.

So, for example, if you have too much Air, you have what is called a Vata imbalance. Think about the implications of having too much Air, Firefly. While on the surface the idea of having too much Air might seem incomprehensible, if you put on your Night-goggles and feel it through, you'll quickly realize an overly aerated person might be dried out, agitated, and prone to overthinking.

Air means something slightly different in Ayurveda than it does in the humoral system. Ayurvedic Air might better be called Wind: it encompasses the principles of motion and restlessness, and it's decidedly dry, whereas in humoral medicine, Air is a bit more of a miasma: humid, warm, and damp.

(While there is a definite sense of simultaneous discovery with the various elemental systems, it would be a mistake to think they're all the same. Remember, just as your lens into the world is colored by your experiences and beliefs, the lenses of the people coming up with these theories were also influenced by their own lives and environments. If you live on a mountain where the air blows in cold and dry, you'll have a different experience of Air than someone who lives on a bayou where the air sits on you like a warm, wet cat.)

China

In the Chinese Wu Xing system the elements are Earth, Air, Fire, Metal, and Wood. Instead of thinking of the elements as ingredients or component parts of all things, the Chinese system saw each as an energy that created transformation. This is very much in line with how the Arabic and medieval alchemists began using the elements centuries later.

(Could there have been an intellectual exchange between the Chinese thinkers and the early Arabic alchemists? Absolutely. The Middle East was a cultural crossroads. Ideas, as well as alembics, would have been enthusiastically bartered and exchanged.)

Let's take a closer look at the Wu Xing system.

The five energies were based on what was seen seasonally in nature and went (very simplistically) like this:

* Water is the potential for new life buried in the cold, dark ground beneath the snows of winter.

* Wood is the outward stretching of new growth as it emerges from the earth in the spring.

* Fire is the process of maturation that takes place in the heat of the summer sun.

* Earth is the ripening of fruits and grains in late summer fields.

* Metal is the autumn harvest and the collecting and storing of seeds so that a new cycle can begin.

The cycle of changes maps out how these energies behave in nature. Fire consumes Wood and turns it into Earth. Earth freezes and thaws, trapping Water. Water rusts Metal. Metal cuts Wood. It's kind of like a cosmological game of rock, paper, scissors.

In other systems, you could think of each element as a noun, but in the Five Element system, each element is a verb: it is doing and changing, not just being. Each of us has an element that we're working with in this lifetime, learning through the changes and transmutations our particular element goes through:

* Wood loves growth and freedom, but may get stymied by stagnation or feeling stuck, which leads to anger and frustration.

* Fire dances between joy and desolation—the captivating flame to the dull ember—and learns the emotional spectrum from control to surrender.

* Metal is the Lancelot of the elements: it focuses on purity and honor. Lancelot moves from loss and longing through communion, feeling everything deeply but showing little on the surface.

* Water's work is to flow from self-doubt toward faith and trust (and sometimes back again); when a Water person is out of balance, they slip into fear.

* Earthy people move from gratitude and completeness to lack and overthinking. They're our elemental worriers, the Earth Mamas who want to make sure everyone's made it home safely after a Night out stargazing.

I'm fascinated by the Five Element system because, unlike the classic Greek or Ayurvedic elemental systems, both of which tell you what *is*, the Five Element system shows you the cycle, illuminating not only what is but, through elemental transformation, *what will be*.

And there you have it, Firefly, divination everywhere!

Despite their differences, all the element-based medicinal systems—whether Ayurvedic or Unani Tibb or Tibetan—make intuitive sense. Even without being versed in the specifics, when we relax into our Night-vision, we can understand the metaphors.

Homework: Chart Your Elements

Tonight, your work is to explore your personal elemental makeup!

You can choose which system you'd like to experiment with: Ayurvedic or Wu Xing. For both, you can find online quizzes to determine your constitutional type. (The English language search term for Wu Xing is "five element" so look up "five elements quiz.") While these quizzes aren't perfect, you'll learn all sorts of things about yourself, including the best foods to eat for your constitution and, depending on the quiz, which colors to wear to boost your elemental balance.

Keep in mind that your Ayurvedic dosha is meant to be a description of the elements that make up your being, while your Five Element constitutional type describes the changes and transformations you are working with in this lifetime. They are complementary theories so you might want to explore both.

A quiz is a great starting point to give you ideas for the types of things you'll want to think about when determining your inner elemental makeup. But don't let any quiz have the final say, Firefly: feel into yourself and see what you notice about *you*. Allow each of the elements to roll around on your tongue and decide which tastes you prefer: the mellow magic of Earth or the sharp heat of Fire? The burble of Water or the poof of Air? Does what you prefer balance you or mirror you?

ADDITIONAL READINGS AND RESOURCES

When I sat down to map out these lesson plans, Firefly, I didn't reach for *Mrs. Pennyworth's Guide to Mistressing the Elements* or even *Spagyrics: The Alchemical Preparation of Medicinal Essences, Tinctures, and Elixirs* by Manfred Junius.

No.

Instead I went to the cookbook section of my library and pulled out Michael Pollan's *Cooked* and Samin Nosrat's *Salt, Fat, Acid, Heat*. It can feel disembodying to read theory and instructions on how to do things you know you aren't actually going to do. But I know I'm going to cook. Perhaps you cook, too? The kitchen can be an incredible laboratory to explore the way that Earth, Air, Water, and Fire actually operate in the world.

If you want to go a step further and explore the elements through alchemical experiments, *Spagyrics: The Alchemical Preparation of Medicinal Essences, Tinctures, and Elixirs* does have instructions and so does *Real Alchemy* by Robert Bartlett.

If you want to see how simultaneous invention serendipitously plays out in real time, check out Elizabeth Gilbert's *Big Magic*, where she talks about free-range ideas on the search for their person.

You can explore how the elements have been used in medicine across Asian, North African, and European cultures by researching:

* **Five Element Theory: Chinese & Taoist**

* **Bön: Tibetan**

* **Ayurvedic Doshas: Hindu (the elements are mentioned in the classic text of the Vedas)**

* **Unani Tibb: Arabic**

* **Humoral system: Classic Greek and early European**

For a greater understanding of how the elements affect living spaces, research feng shui and Vastu Shastra.

For a take on the elements in modern magic, read Scott Cunningham's *Earth, Air, Fire, and Water: More Techniques of Natural Magic*. Donald Michael Kraig's *Modern Magick: Eleven Lessons in the High Magickal Arts* walks you through ceremonial magic, in which the four elements play a starring role. And Starhawk's *The Spiral Dance: A Rebirth of the Ancient Religion of the Great Goddess* works with the elements through the lens of Earth-based spirituality.

Richard Morris's *The Last Sorcerers—The Path from Alchemy to the Periodic Table* takes you on an enjoyable jaunt through the history of science. While well researched, some people have even called this book "romantic."

While it's hard to find English translations of the works of Muhammad ibn Umail al-Tamimi, you can peruse C. G. Jung's *Modern Man in Search of a Soul* and *Psychology and Alchemy* to deep dive into using alchemy for personal transformation.

The classics on this topic are dense and hard to get through. If you want a little daylight reading (perhaps after a bit of caffeine), try Aristotle's *On the Heavens*, or Plato's dialogue called *Timaeus* in which he describes the Platonic solids, which are based on the elements.

If you are mathematically minded, Euclid's *Elements* is a classic. (I've never even attempted this one, Firefly.) Remember, Aristotle and Co. were looking for the elements as the smallest parts of the whole. Euclid lays out the mathematical systems that govern the elements. This is sometimes called one of the most influential books ever written, so if your brain works in geometries, it is well worth a read.

harnessing the celestial tides

(Energetic
Engineering 101)

LET'S GET YOU ORIENTED TO THE CELESTIAL HAPPENINGS
in the Night sky, Firefly. To do so, we're going to head outdoors and perform a little magic trick.

But before you stroll into the Night, I need you to do something that may seem a little odd. I'll explain why in just a minute but, for now, live in the mystery and look up the latitude of the place where you're currently located. If you're in New York City, for example, your latitude is 40.7 degrees. If you happen to be in Paris, please visit the boulangerie on rue Jean-Pierre Timbaud, enjoy a sourdough baguette for me, and know that you are at 48.85 degrees latitude.

(If you're in the Southern Hemisphere, you're going to have to enjoy this particular magic on paper, because what we're about to do won't actually work in your Night sky. *C'est la vie, non?*)

Once you have your latitude, grab your compass, and let's go for a walk under the stars. You'll need to be able to actually read your compass, *mon cherie*, so if it's a dark Night, be sure to bring a light.

Find a spot that's at least a little bit dark. If you're in the countryside, that's fairly easy; if you're in the city, move away from the streetlights and the giant, neon signboards: this won't work standing in the middle of Times Square.

Once you're in relative darkness, use your compass to find north. Turn yourself so you're facing that direction.

In order to perform this magic trick, we need to do a little mental geometry:

In your mind, draw a giant arc over your head, stretching from north to south. You can picture it like a starry rainbow, with one end directly behind you in the south and the pot of gold in front of you in the north. Now, even if you can't see the horizon line, imagine that you can. In your mind, assign the northern horizon the number zero and the southern horizon, the other end of the rainbow, 180. These numbers represent degrees, Firefly, like on a protractor. If zero is the northern horizon, and 180 is the southern horizon, then 90 degrees is directly over your head. Orient yourself by figuring out, approximately, where 45 degrees is: find the spot directly between 90 degrees and the northern horizon. Once you've got it, it's time for the magic.

Ready?

Remember that number I had you look up? The latitude of your current location? Take that number (40.7 degrees for NYC, 48.85 for Paris) and look up from the northern horizon until your eyes find the spot in the sky that, in your rough estimation, matches the latitude of your location. In that spot (or very close) there should be a very bright star. That star's name is Polaris, the North Star.

People have been navigating by Polaris since people began navigating. The Mongolians called it the peg that holds the world together. The Norse saw it as the shining tip of the spike around which the entire sky rotates. Congratulations, Firefly, you just joined a long lineage of sailors and itinerant travelers who have been looking up at the Night sky to help them orient and find their way. For millennia the sky was not only stellar, it was useful. Every Night, a map and a calendar were scrawled across the heavens. The Night sky told you not only *where* you were, but also *when* you were.

Ancient you would find the North Star and be able to roughly calculate your current latitude, then ancient you would glance at the eastern horizon to see what constellation was rising. "Oh!" ancient you would say, "I left Amiens this morning. I'm now at 48 degrees latitude and Taurus is on the eastern horizon. That means I'm getting close to Paris and it's some time near the winter solstice." *Wait!* you might be thinking. *How is Taurus in the sky at the winter solstice? I thought Taurus was the star sign for May?* Ah, *mon cherie*, you'll want to grab a *chocolat chaud* to enjoy with your baguette, this is going to take some explaining . . . Which I will do in your coming lessons!

SYLLABUS

One of the oldest forms of divination is astrology—you can't understand the Night without it! This course traces the history of stargazing, exploring the ways in which people have used the stars for divination across a myriad of cultures.

Why, you might wonder, is this important? It's only by returning to the roots from which astrology grew that we can gain a deeper understanding of how this system of stargazing relates to our own lives. These ancient star stories are sprinkled through the oldest spaces of the C.U. and are quietly influencing our world to this day.

Astrology itself is a lifetime study: this course is an *amuse-bouche* to whet your appetite. We'll tour through the conceptions of the Night sky that created our modern theories of astrology and gaze lovingly upon the macro-level patterns used in astrological divination.

In fact, you can consider this course a tapas bar of delectable tidbits, culminating in suggestions for deepening your personal work with the Night sky's patterns and cycles. Your final lessons will include following the patterns of the moon to get you accustomed to viewing your life through the lens of celestial cycles, giving you a basis for understanding the longer cycles of the stars. This is something best learned through experience, so be ready to feast on a moon-th long homework assignment. You'll be taking a turn through the energies of the moon's phases, in order to know them intimately. That way, you'll be able to incorporate lunar knowledge into your Night-workings immediately: the moon, the celestial body closest to Earth, makes stellar training wheels for beginning to divine the larger patterns and movements of the constellations.

Topics include:

LESSON 1:	When Earth Was the Center of the Universe
LESSON 2:	Home of the Gods
LESSON 3:	The Clock in the Sky
LESSON 4:	A Quick Trip in a Supersonic Jet
LESSON 5:	Way Finding via the Stars
LESSON 6:	Tropical or Sidereal?
LESSON 7:	The Quadrants
LESSON 8:	Make It Personal
LESSON 9:	The Celestial Stewpot
LESSON 10:	Scrying the Stars
LESSON 11:	Harnessing the Lunar Tides
LESSON 12:	The Cycle of Return

Note: In the coming evenings, you'll hear me referring to Babylonian, Hellenistic, and Vedic astrology, quadrants in the sky, and seasonal elements. It's a lot! And you don't need to know it all. As you are working through the coming lessons, keep two things in mind:

* **There are many systems of astrology and even different zodiacs used around the world.**

* **There's a resource section at the end of the course chock-full of helpful material.**

As always, take your time. Allow the lessons to percolate in your Night-brain. (Percolation makes the best coffee, and I suspect it also makes the most significant thoughts. Just let yourself be water, Firefly, and bubble your way through these grounds over and over.)

Homework should be turned in to your journal 72 hours after it is assigned. Try marking your lesson complete using the current phase of the moon. Don't know the current moon phase? No worries! This will be noted on your ephemeris (remember I mentioned in your supply list that you'd be wanting one?) or you could just say, "Hey Siri! What's tonight's moon phase?" and she'll hook you up with an answer. This will begin the habit of following La Luna on her moon-thly trek through the Night sky.

Lesson 1:

WHEN EARTH WAS THE CENTER OF THE UNIVERSE

Light a candle and settle in, Firefly: we have miles to go before we sleep! We'll begin with *once upon a time.*

> Once upon a time, the Earth thought she was the center of the universe . . .

If you think you're the center of everything, you're called *egocentric.* Back when Earth thought she was the center of the universe, she was called *geocentric* (*geo* from the Greek meaning "earth or land"; and *centric* from the Greek meaning "full of yourself").

You can't really blame Earth for thinking the universe revolved around her: everyone told her that she was the center point, the nexus, and the beating heart of all that mattered. Neither can you find fault with the people living on Earth: from the vantage point of Yinxu or Babylon, it certainly looked like Earth was the hub, with the sun circling around her, rising and setting each day, and, further out, the stars kicking up their heels as they cycled through the seasons.

Geocentrism was a beautiful misconception (we've seen any number of those, haven't we, Firefly?), which formed the basis of our relationship to the cosmos for millennia. We now look up at the sky knowing that we live on a spherical-shaped planet, rotating around an average-sized sun. (Truth be told, Sol is a bit . . . *petite.*) The round rubber-ball shape of our planet has been established for centuries. We can even call up photos, taken from space, affirming this deduction.

It's hard to imagine what our earliest ancestors saw when they looked up at the heavens. It was essentially the same sky, but our understanding of the universe has shifted exponentially in the intervening eons. For millennia, people looked up and they didn't *know*. It was all a mystery, and as with the other mysteries we've explored, both theories and stories abounded. What united all of them—across cultures and continents—was that each of these beautiful misconceptions had Earth at its center.

My favorite of these lovely fallacies is the cosmology developed by the pre-Socratic philosopher Anaximander, in which the Earth was a cylinder, like a kaleidoscope. (Picture the stars spinning round as the tube twists!) Which wasn't exactly what Anaximander envisioned: his Earth-cylinder floated within a series of wheels, and those wheels had pinholes poked in them. The planets, sun, and moon were, in Anaximander's model, peepholes into the fiery universe beyond the wheels.

This idea of wheels or celestial spheres was a prevalent train of thought at the time, and both Plato and the entirety of the Chinese Hun Tian school were on board. Other theories involved domes, voids, and the swirling skirts of a dancing goddess. (I made that last one up, Firefly, but my Night-brain knows that, in some forgotten past, someone believed it.) The Night sky was the place of stories and speculation. The lack of knowing allowed for a kind of magic we've nearly forgotten: *mystery.*

Homework: Write a Stellar Story

Let's imagine a different kind of Night sky than most of us experience, Firefly:

This Night sky has a swirl of stars, so many stars there hardly seems to be space between them. The brightest stars look like sharp pinpricks, while the faintest blur together to form a fabric of shimmering light, which seems to undulate just a little. The sky itself feels like it's curving overhead in an almost-visible dome above you. Tonight is the Night of the dark moon (even if it isn't, it is in our visualization, Firefly): there are no other lights in the sky beyond those swirling stars.

You lie on your back, staring up. The modern world falls away. Maybe it's 2,000 years ago . . . maybe two million. It's just you, the Earth at your back, and the stars above.

If you were this person, lying under this timeless sky, with no knowledge of Nicolaus Copernicus's heliocentric theory (that's the one that put the sun at the center of our universe) or the astronauts of Apollo 11 doing a moon walk, what story might you tell about the stars and their relationship to the Earth and to you?

Lesson 2:

HOME OF THE GODS

The first thing that ancient cultures agreed upon was that Earth was the center of the universe. (Earth liked this, and it was good.) But there was a second global synchronicity, a story or belief that came in a variety of ensembles. When you were told this story, or had this belief explained, the exact details of it were nuanced by its culture of origin. But this tale—no matter how it was told—knew itself, at its heart, to be one story wearing a variety of fancy hats and wigs and occasionally a star-swept skirt.

The simplest version of that story is this: *the gods live in the heavens.*

Homework: Listen to the Stories

Choose three ancient cultures from different parts of the globe and read a few of their earliest tales. (Need ideas? Try Babylonian, Maori, and Tibetan. Or Phoenician, Aztec, and Mongolian.) Pay attention to where the people live and where the gods reside. Look for the principle of *as above, so below* in action. Scan for dualities as you sieve for synchronicities.

How did these stories impact the ways in which people thought about the Night sky when they were standing under it, looking up?

Lesson 3:

THE CLOCK IN THE SKY

The Night sky was the GPS—global positioning system—of its time. Understanding the scope of GPS will give you an idea of how important the Night sky used to be. (Don't get indignant about my indulgence in modern electronics, Firefly. With the exception of orienting on Polaris to stop by the boulangerie and buy me a baguette, when was the last time you stood outside, looked up, and actually *used* the stars to find your way in the world?)

Just like GPS, the Night sky was used by the ancients to provide positioning, navigation, and timing . . . and these services were as integrated into ancient society as GPS is in our lives today. Essentially, what we're talking about is knowing where you are in time and space. Tonight, we'll tackle time. We'll get to aspects of positioning and navigation (the spatial portion) in just a few evenings.

GPS has been described as a "vast, spaceborne clock" (Bloomberg Businessweek), but the ancients probably would have scratched their heads at its necessity, knowing they already had a vast, spaceborne clock. It was called the Night sky. As you'll see in the next lesson, they created earthborne timekeeping devices simply to track and record the Sky Clock's missives.

The Clock in the Sky provided the markers that we humans used to define the growing season here on planet Earth. These were called the solstices and equinoxes. (The plural of equinox is technically *equinoctes*, Firefly, but I suspect you would think I "typoed" if I used equinoctes in a sentence.) In addition to reminding people when to sow and when to harvest, the Sky Clock kept religious observances ticking along at the proper moment. Time was kept by tracking moon cycles between the equinoxes and solstices, combined with counting full moons and noting moon phase. Instead of putting a date at the top of the page when you wrote in your journal, you would write something like *three days after the full moon* or *in the time of the longest Nights*.

While ancient timekeeping might seem crude—or romantic, depending on your mood—it gave rise to a number of calendar systems that worked fairly well, especially when you remember that our current system only works flawlessly because of a well-timed leap.

The earliest Egyptian calendar was lunar, as were many ancient systems. But simply following the lunar cycles failed to help the Egyptians predict a very important event: the annual flooding of the Nile. While La Luna wasn't forthcoming with this vital information, the Egyptians had begun to notice that the Dog Star (that's a star called Sirius, which is in the constellation Canis Major, Firefly) was reliably predictive: the Nile flooded just a few days after the Dog Star appeared right before sunrise. This sent the ancient Egyptians searching for a better system. They decided to follow the sun and, as far as we know, were the first to move to a mainly solar year. They devised a 365-day calendar (sound familiar?) which came into use in 4236 BCE, making that year the earliest one recorded in history.

The Egyptians weren't the only peoples to turn to the stars to predict important events in their calendar year. The Zuni peoples of New Mexico used the Pleiades cluster—which they called the Seed Stars—as an agricultural calendar. When the Seed Stars faded in the western sky at dusk in the spring, they knew they were past the last frost date and it was safe to plant seeds. They kept an eye out for the reappearance of the Seed Stars in the east, just before sunrise, because this marked when planting needed to be completed for the shoots to mature before the first frost.

The biggest issue the older calendar systems faced, regardless of where on Earth they were being conceived, was that a year of the Night sky didn't quite align with a year of the day sky. (And doesn't that provide any number of nifty rabbit holes for both of our brains to go down?) Trying to reconcile the lunar year (we have 13 full moons in a lunar year, Firefly) with the solar year, which is roughly 365 days, got us some whack-a-doodle systems. If you do a little math, you'll see that it's not an easy problem to solve. The Babylonians tried, with a calendar composed of alternate 29-day and 30-day months. This managed to keep vaguely in sync with the lunar year. To loop in the solar year, they added an extra month three times every eight years. This rather unorthodox trick sort of worked, but over time the accumulated differences between the solar and lunar year would need reckoning. This required the king to decree an extra month, which he did whenever he felt like the calendar had fallen too out of step with the seasons.

This need to manipulate the calendars to make them work became, over time, politicized. People, being people, found ways to use "fixing the calendar" to their own advantage: *I'm head priest until the end of the year? Um, I think we need to add six months into the current year in order to make the calendar work.* Yes, that type of thing really did happen. Just another historical true story.

But I digress. Let's travel forward a bit in time, Firefly, and see what comes next:

In 48 BCE, Julius Caesar asked the astronomer Sosigenes to create a calendar that didn't need constant fixing. The result? A calendar with 365 days and months of 30 to 31 days, with a leap year every fourth year. But over time, this calendar, too, got out of kilter, skipping ahead of the seasons. So in 1582, Pope Gregory VIII fixed the calendar by continuing to add a leap year every fourth year, *except* during century years not evenly divisible by the number 400, known as centurial or secular years. (I'll bet you a sourdough baguette you didn't know that!) This is the calendar we still use today.

While the history of the calendar is fascinating, what I want you to see is the slow but inexorable move from *Let's look at the sky every Night, watch the movement of the stars, and from those cycles get a feel for where we are in the year* to *This calendar stuff is really complicated so I'm going to leave it to the astronomers and mathematicians.* GPS drastically changed our relationship, both individually and culturally, with the Night sky.

Time used to be something we engaged with and observed for ourselves: we walked outside and checked the Clock in the Sky. Now, time is a concept we all collectively believe in. Taking the time to explore the all-encompassing importance of celestial movements to civilizations past (the very civilizations that developed the concepts of astrology we use today) can help you begin to see that contemplating your relationship with the stars was, at its core, about understanding your own life against the backdrop of both time and space (and one other thing . . . but I'm going to play my cards close and let that thing remain a mystery for now!).

To be clear, the exploration of the Night sky wasn't just happening in one part of the world. The Muses love distributing their inspiration widely and generously. The precepts of ancient stargazing were being simultaneously or near simultaneously discovered around the globe.

To prove it, let's take a field trip!

(Bring your homework with you, Firefly, there will be time between flyovers.)

Homework: Let the Moon Be Your Pocket Watch

Research how the moon used to mark the hours of the Night. And, when you're not taking a world tour on a supersonic jet, give it a try!

Lesson 4:

A QUICK TRIP IN A SUPERSONIC JET

Pretend for just a moment that we have a supersonic, invisible jet.

(Why does it need to be invisible? So you can look down and see the splendor below, instead of gazing upon metal and rivets! But if you'd feel safer, Firefly, you can instead imagine a regular plane for this quick gallop around the globe.)

Since we've been spending so much time in Paris, we'll fly out of Charles de Gaulle. The pilot announces our itinerary: we'll head southeast, buzzing over Malta (that's a tiny island between Tunisia and the tip of Italy's boot), and then continue on to Egypt. From there we'll head east to Cambodia (it's a supersonic jet, so it won't take too long), then cross the Pacific to the Americas. We'll visit Mexico and a small town in Illinois just across the border from St. Louis before doing the transatlantic crossing. Our final stop will be Stonehenge, and then I'll drop you back in Paris in time for breakfast.

Why the world tour? you ask. The best way to understand cultural history is to see it. Our archaeoastronomical flyby will familiarize you with some of the most mind-boggling complexes humans have created. The places we're visiting are living calendars, ritual spaces, and maps of the known universe, all writ large upon the landscape. Seeing their monolithic grandeur for yourself will illustrate the importance of the stars to our ancestors better than my words ever could.

So find your invisible seat belt, and buckle up! First stop: Malta.

Not much is known about the people who created the Mnajdra temple complex on Malta. What we do know is that around 3600 BCE, those folks were hauling huge, buff-colored stones into place and decorating them with a zillion little circles, which look like the stars of the Night sky. At sunrise on the equinoxes the sun shines through the main passageway of the temple, unrolling like a flaming carpet to illuminate a small inner shrine.

Can you imagine that, instead of checking the date on your phone, you could instead stroll by this temple complex in the morning, maybe on your way to harvest grapes or prune your olive trees, and check to see how close the sun's light was to the central corridor? This would tell you how close you were to the autumn equinox: the end of the harvest, when the Nights turn cold. You would look at these buildings, knowing generations of your ancestors had worked together to move these rocks into place to provide you with this seasonal knowledge. Perhaps you would feel a sense of continuity and timelessness . . .

. . . Or perhaps I'm just a hopeless romantic.

Either way, keep in mind the time (often centuries), engineering know-how, and sheer willpower it took to construct these astro-calendar temples. The scale of these projects is something we just don't see today.

As we leave the Mnajdra temple behind and continue southeast, you'll quickly see our next destination rising from the horizon. First the Great Pyramid will come into view, quickly followed by the Pyramid of Khafre and the Pyramid of Menkaure. If you look carefully, you'll see the Sphinx, as well.

It's been speculated that the pyramids at Giza, which we are currently flying over, are situated to replicate Orion's sector of sky, which was thought to be the home of the gods. Some say the Giza complex was meant to create heaven on Earth: the three pyramids are aligned in such a way that they mirror Orion's belt, and the Nile River becomes the Milky Way, with the Sphinx representing the constellation Leo.

Is it *true*? Is this what the ancient Egyptians intended? The daytime world may never know, but the Night recognizes its own truths.

Let's follow the Nile south so we can swing past the Temple of Amun at Karnak. During the summer and winter solstices, the sun shines all the way through the length of the temple to beam into the central room, which is dedicated to Amun, the god of sun and air. Karnak (which is the temple's modern name—the ancients called this place *Nesut-Towi*, "Throne of the Two Lands" and *Ipetsut*, "The Most Select of Places") was constructed over the course of 2,000 years, beginning around 2055 BCE. Some say it is the largest religious complex in the world, but Angkor Wat contests that claim. We'll head there next and you can decide for yourself.

(Babylonia, the jewel in the crown of ancient Mesopotamia, should be next on our itinerary, Firefly, but, alas, there are no archaeoastronomy sites to visit. Ancient Mesopotamia has been conquered and reconquered for millennia: war takes more of a toll than time, not only on people, but on structures. The extensive records kept by the Babylonian astronomers directly influenced the astronomical theories in the Hellenistic, Hindu, and Islamic worlds. In many ways, modern astronomy and both Western and Hindu astrology are a part of the legacy of astronomer-priests of Mesopotamia.)

Since we won't be stopping in Babylonia, we'll head straight to one of my favorite stargazing spots on the planet: Angkor Wat, Cambodia. The complex here is part of what might be considered a second wave of astroarchaeological sites, constructed between 1113 and 1150 CE. Built to honor the Hindu god Vishnu (Angkor Wat became a Buddhist temple in the 12th century), the complex is also a vast observatory that showcases both the solstices and equinoxes, as well as lunar alignments. (I'll tuck the name of an article with details in the Additional Resources section if you want to know more.) This is one I wish you could experience at ground level, Firefly. Even during tourist season, there's a joyful peace here. From a distance, the turrets and towers are dramatic, but up close, it's all timeworn stone and greenery framing the bright flare of the monks' saffron-dyed robes as they perch atop the walls.

Are you beginning to see, Firefly, how universal the tracking of celestial events has been?

If we had more time we could zip north to China, which had its own highly sophisticated system of calendaring. In terms of development, the Chinese calendar mirrors the time frame of Egypt's. It's worth noting that while in modern times astronomers are considered scientists and astrologers are seen as Night-besotted dreamers, in ancient China both of these positions were respected. In fact, China is one of the few ancient cultures that distinguished between the two: astronomy was a secular study whose domain was mapping the stars, while astrology was concerned with divination and interpretation of the will of the gods based on the movement of the stars as indicated by the astronomers. An interesting division of labor to contemplate as we zip across the Pacific to the Americas.

We'll begin at the Mayan ruin of Chichen Itza in Mexico. The El Castillo pyramid there was built in 1000 CE as a tribute to Kukulcan, the serpent deity. At sunset on the autumn and spring equinoxes, the cleverly constructed, and precisely calculated, architecture creates a serpent of light, which slithers down the pyramid's steps to reach the carved snake head of Kukulcan. Speaking of calendars, the Mayans resolved the pesky problems others were having by using three calendars simultaneously!

There are dozens more sites to the south, but we're going to head north, to better align us for the last leg of our journey. We'll need to buzz in low to see our next site. It's a circle of cedar posts, reconstructed in 1985, and affectionately called Woodhenge. Located at the Cahokia Mounds in the state of Illinois, in the area that is currently the United States, Woodhenge was built and rebuilt first by the Mississippian people and then the Cahokia people; the posts mark the summer and winter solstices as well as the spring and autumn equinoxes, serving a similar purpose as the last stop on our tour, Stonehenge.

As we zip across the Atlantic, Firefly, I want to caution you about thinking that all these sites are the same. They are . . . and they're not: moths and cats are drawn to light for entirely different reasons. Each of these stellar places has a specific history tied to both the culture that created it and the people who continued to use the site over the centuries, adjusting the traditions for their own changing times.

Our final stop is Stonehenge in England. There are a number of archaeoastronomical sites around the British Isles (and even some that are older), but this is the most famous. The megalithic dolmen at Stonehenge mark the passage of the sun at the summer and winter solstices. Like the pyramids, their construction boggles the modern mind: how was this achieved without cranes and trucks and paved highways? We forget that our ancestors took a longer view of time than we do today. These were generational projects, and their building often spanned multiple

human lifetimes. They were considered worthy long-term endeavors precisely because the stars, and how they guided our lives both physically and metaphorically, were vital in ways that I hope you are beginning to feel deep in your Night bones.

As we reenter Paris airspace, look down on the glass pyramid at the Louvre, designed by Chinese American I.M. Pei. It seems a fitting denouement for our journey, doesn't it, Firefly? Perhaps that glass pyramid's construction was the beginning of a new long cycle of time that people a millennia from now will fly over on their world tour.

Homework: Take a Ground-Level Tour

Choose one of the sites we flew over—or one that we didn't—and dig in! Learn the basics (you know, Firefly: *the who, what, where, and when* of it). Then go deeper:

* What was the connection between the site and a sense of the divine or sacred?

* What was the connection to time and the calendar?

* How was the site originally used and how has that evolved over time?

Lesson 5:

WAY FINDING VIA THE STARS

We've already dipped a cookie into how the stars were used for actual navigation. But there's more to "way finding" than simply locating the bakery, Firefly. The Night sky was also used for finding your way through life by divining the future: you looked up so you could see what *your stars* were doing.

That's right, Firefly, you had your own stars.

And you still do.

And this, *mon amie*, is the beginning of our exploration of what we today call astrology.

This idea of the stars being predictive evolved in a way that is a head-scratcher from a modern point of view: the first things the stars were used to predict were the seasons. *Huh?* you might think. *Why would anyone need divination for that?* It's hard to conceive of a time before calendars, Firefly, but such a time existed (which is why cultures across the globe dragged large rocks into formations that helped them to read the stars) and "astrology" (in quotes because it is so different from our modern version) helped predict things like when to plant seeds and when to harvest the grain. And, because there was no chance to run down to Mama Glendock's Country Market to fetch some eggs and a bit of spinach for dinner, these divinations—the ones that said when to plant the spinach seeds and when to get the chickens indoors for the Night—were life-and-death predictions. The stars, it would seem, knew everything.

It's not such a leap then, to begin looking for personal futures in the position of the celestial bodies. Folks in ancient Egypt had just as much of a desire as we do to understand the course their lives would take. And who doesn't want to know when they might fall in love or come into a bit of luck? Thus, the idea of personal horoscopes was conceived.

There are 21 places around the globe that are not in the country of Egypt, but are nevertheless called Egypt. If you grew up in one of these new Egypts, like Egypt, Arkansas, or Egypt, North Carolina, you likely think of horoscopes as the 12 tidy tidbits, one for each star sign, provided by magazines and online sites as a bit of amusement. You might shrug them off, thinking *how accurate can they be if they apply to 1/12th of the population?*

Let's clear up a common misconception, Firefly: a 12th of the population does *not* have the same horoscope as you. Your astrological chart is like a cosmic fingerprint—similar to that of others, but absolutely unique. At the exact moment when you inhaled your way into the world, the stars were in a specific spot (or, to be more accurate, the Earth was in a specific spot in relation to the heavens). Further, how those stars appeared in the sky above your newborn head was particular to the locale of your birth. So, while the stars were in a specific setup at 9:28 a.m., they would look different if you were in Poughkeepsie (that's New York) instead of Port Harcourt (that's Nigeria). The only person who could possibly share a star chart with you is another baby who entered the world in precisely the same location, at exactly the same moment in time—which is possible, but relatively unlikely.

So when ancient you came crying and wailing into the world, the priests and the wisewomen of the original Egypt walked outside and looked at the stars, examining their position in the hour of your birth. And the sky did its part, telling the entire story of who you might become. The pattern spangled across the heavens was *yours* . . . or, perhaps, you were the sky's, an imperfect human reflection of the heavens at the moment you were born. As above, so below.

Okay, Firefly, I'm ready to lay that final card on the table, the one I've held on to because it is both infinitely important to understanding astrology but also rankles our modern sensibilities. I've mentioned this once, but I suspect you blew by it, thinking it was just the Night Mistress getting sidetracked.

Here it is again:

The gods lived in the heavens.

The Night sky was their domain. So, when the priests and the wise-women were staring upward in the hour of your birth, what they were scrying for was what the gods had to say about your sudden appearance on this planet.

These are the circumstances under which astrology, as a system, was created. This sense of the Night sky holding knowledge of time and place and the will of the gods is all baked into the cosmic cake.

Homework: The Stars, the Gods, and You

The idea that the gods live in the heavens and use the Night sky as a bill-board to display their approval or displeasure, teach a cultural or moral lesson, or foretell a coming event, can seem both whimsical and overbearing. We modern humans give a worthy display of opposite extremes every time someone says a word like *god, destiny, predetermined,* and *fate.* On the one hand, we want to go to the astrologer or tarot reader to see what comes next, while on the other we want to be the mistresses of our own destiny. Free will is not up for discussion.

What if you don't have to remove this internal tension? What if you can simply accept the oppositions within yourself?

If you're feeling like you can accept a little fate and some deity-based divination, do some research on your astrological Sun sign. (Your Sun sign is the one tied to the month of your birth.) Are there stories associated with it? Does it have a ruling god or goddess? What might the message written on the sky have been in the moment you popped into earthly existence?

Lesson 6:

TROPICAL OR SIDEREAL?

Warning: You are entering a daylight zone. The concepts in lesson 6 are brain twisters.

So why include them at all?

Besides nourishing the noggins of the mathematically inclined, this lesson shows off the complexities and nuances of astrology, as well as the contortions that have occurred over the millennia it's been practiced.

A number of highly intelligent people have worked through this lesson and come out looking like they were whipped in a Vitamix. Unless you geek out on conflicting calendars and coordinate planes, I recommend skipping to lesson 7.

If you're skipping ahead, here are your takeaways:

* Different cultures use divergent models of the heavens in their astrology. Western astrology uses *tropical*. Vedic (the astrology associated with the Hindu religion and the country of India) uses *sidereal*.

* Every once in a while, an astronomer says, "Don't believe astrology! The constellations have shifted in the sky since it was invented, so if it ever worked, it doesn't work anymore." It is true that the constellations have shifted in their actual positions. It's also true that a smart guy name Ptolemy made adjustments for this two thousand years ago.

* Finally, the constellation of Taurus is in the Night sky in December. In late April and May, which are associated with Taurus, it is in the day sky, hidden behind the bright light of the sun, which is why we say, "the sun is in Taurus." That may already seem a bit confusing, but it's actually even more complex than this . . .

* Proving my final point: astrology is complicated and intricate.

If you're happy enough with these easy, but incomplete, answers and want to preserve your brain cells, hop over to lesson 7.

If you're ready to do some mental pull-ups, crank up your astrolabe and continue on!

While the signs of the zodiac were identified as early as 700 BCE by the Babylonians, they were used, at that point, to predict the changing seasons, not to determine whether you should study embalming in Alexandria or metallurgy in Ur. The system the Babylonians developed divided the sky into 12 quadrants, each named for the constellation that, at that time, was housed there. Each of those quadrants measured 30 degrees. A bit of quick math will confirm that 30 × 12 is 360, or the number of degrees in a circle. So these evenly spaced quadrants formed the circle that the sun perambulated around the Earth—which was still, at this point, the center of the universe.

Do you remember, way back at the beginning of this course when you were doing your North Star and compass exercise, that I mentioned that Taurus was in the Night sky around the winter solstice? And you thought I was crazy, because Taurus is the constellation associated with the month of May? Here's where we unravel that particular mystery!

In May, the sun is in Taurus. And, I know this next thing I'm going to say is obvious, Firefly, but it must be said for this to all make sense: we can only see the sun during the day. So in May, the sun, during the day, is in the sign of Taurus—but we can't see the constellation itself, because the sun is too bright. If you picture a cosmic lineup, first comes Earth, then the sun, and then Taurus, hanging like wallpaper on the far side of the sun. This is what we mean when we say, "the sun is in Taurus."

Constellations North of the Band of the Zodiac

AQUARIUS CAPRICORN SAGITTARIUS SCORPIO LIBRA

PISCES

EARTH ——— SUN

THE BAND OF THE ZODIAC

ARIES TAURUS GEMINI CANCER LEO VIRGO

Constellations South of the Band of the Zodiac

When the sun is in Taurus, what you see when you look at the Night sky is the quadrant of the cosmos that is exactly opposite Taurus or, if you are mathematical, 180 degrees away. So, when the sun is in Taurus, the Scorpio quadrant is actually visible in the Night sky.

This gets us to yet another head-scratcher, Firefly. Notice I said "the Scorpio quadrant," not the constellation of Scorpio.

Over the years since this system was created, the relationship between the actual constellations and the Earth has shifted a bit. So the Scorpio constellation is no longer in the Scorpio quadrant.

But don't panic!

The quadrant system accounts for this. It's meant to be a fixed system based on regions of the sky, which were named after the constellations. Think about it—each of the constellations is a different size, plus there are 13 constellations the sun passes through (the 13th left-out-and-needing-a-little-love constellation is called Ophiuchus). So the designation of exactly 30 degrees per constellation can't be literal: it's instead a systemized version of the Night sky. Or, more accurately, it's a systemized version of the *ecliptic*, which is the name for the path the sun takes through the sky. (The Night sky is decorated with constellations, most of which don't happen to fall in the sun's path at all.) The sun passes through each quadrant of the ecliptic, and each of these quadrants has fixed dates during which the sun is crossing through it. So when you say *I'm a Gemini* or *I'm a Leo*, what you're actually saying is that the sun was visiting the quadrant of that name at the moment of your birth. This is called a tropical zodiac, and it was developed by a guy you may have heard of named Ptolemy (c. 100–c. 170 CE). Having static sectors of the zodiac is a way to make something complex and irregular into a system that's a smidge easier to work with.

If the tropical system doesn't align perfectly with the constellations, what, you might be wondering, does it align with? And the answer is: the equinoxes and solstices. The tropical zodiac begins in the Aries quadrant on the spring equinox and each season has three monthlong quadrants.

But not everyone uses the tropical zodiac. Vedic astrologers diverged from Western astrologers at the point of Ptolemy. They use a system called the sidereal zodiac. The sidereal zodiac also uses 12 signs with 30 degrees each. But it isn't oriented to the seasons—instead it's oriented to the fixed stars, or constellations. Here are the ways that the dates of each zodiac sign shift from the tropical to the sidereal system.

SIGN	SYMBOL	TROPICAL	SIDEREAL
ARIES (Ram)	♈	March 21— April 19	April 15— May 14
TAURUS (Bull)	♉	April 20— May 20	May 15— June 14
GEMINI (Twins)	♊	May 21— June 21	June 15— July 14
CANCER (Crab)	♋	June 22— July 22	July 15— August 14
LEO (Lion)	♌	July 23— August 22	August 15— September 14
VIRGO (Virgin)	♍	August 23— September 22	September 15— October 14
LIBRA (Balance)	♎	September 23— October 23	October 15— November 14
SCORPIO (Scorpion)	♏	October 24— November 21	November 15— December 14
SAGITTARIUS (Archer)	♐	November 22— December 21	December 15— January 14
CAPRICORN (Goat)	♑	December 22— January 19	January 15— February 14
AQUARIUS (Water Bearer)	♒	January 20— February 18	February 15— March 14
PISCES (Fish)	♓	February 19— March 20	March 15— April 14

Finally, for comparison's sake, here are the astronomical dates when the sun crosses through the various constellations (rather than the quadrants) of the ecliptic. And look! I've included our friend Ophiuchus.

Constellation on the Ecliptic Dates When the Sun Crosses It

CAPRICORN	January 21–February 16
AQUARIUS	February 16–March 11
PISCES	March 11–April 18
ARIES	April 18–May 13
TAURUS	May 13–June 22
GEMINI	June 22–July 21
CANCER	July 21–August 10
LEO	August 10–September 16
VIRGO	September 16–October 31
LIBRA	October 31–November 23
SCORPIO	November 23–November 29
OPHIUCHUS	November 29–December 18
SAGITTARIUS	December 18–January 21

Homework: Rest Your Brain . . .

. . . Because that was a lot!

See you tomorrow Night!

THE QUADRANTS

The ancient astrologers divided the Night sky into quadrants like a giant pizza pie. (That's an American pizza pie, Firefly, the round kind. Pizzas in Rome are just as often rectangular, so let's make sure we all have the same image in our heads.) And each of these quadrants was named for a constellation of the zodiac.

From now on, Firefly, I'll just say *zodiac signs* or simply *signs* and you'll know I'm referring to the quadrant, not the constellation.

The quest to make a Theory of Everything never quite abated, and the precept *as above, so below* was still very much in play through the Middle Ages and the Renaissance. Over time, in an effort to have astrology become a Theory of Everything, people loaded up the zodiac signs with added meanings. It's kind of like the ice cream station at a wedding banquet, where you can take a perfectly serviceable bowl of mint chocolate chip and load it up with taste sensations like gummy worms and red hots that may, or may not, create a more delectable dessert. Among the toppings added to the signs were the four elements and, with the advent of medical astrology (which was simply considered part of medicine and not woo-woo at all), parts of the human body. I've included those tidbits in the descriptions below.

Here's the rundown:

ARIES (Fire: cardinal) energetics: Aries is the first sign in the zodiac and brings the energy of the beginning of the cycle—enthusiasm, ambition, spontaneity, choosing change over security, prone to competitiveness, assertiveness, and ambition. In the body: the head—skull, sinuses, and jaw.

TAURUS (Earth: fixed) energetics: security, sensuality, love of functional beauty, stubbornness, and the creation of things that last and increase in value. In the body: neck, throat, tonsils, and thyroid.

GEMINI (Air: mutable) energetics: lively, quick-witted, intellectual, social, inconsistent, fickle, prone to outside influence, dual-natured, creative with communication. In the body: lungs, arms and hands, nervous system.

CANCER (Water: cardinal) energetics: nurturing, nostalgic; focused on home life, family, and emotional rapport; has a tendency to overdo; uncomfortable in unfamiliar surroundings. In the body: breasts, stomach, womb, and liver.

LEO (Fire: fixed) energetics: open, warm, outgoing, social, generous, egotistical, prideful, dramatic, entertaining, emphasis on self, creative energy. In the body: heart, upper back, and spine.

VIRGO (Earth: mutable) energetics: methodical, detail-oriented; focused on organizing, completing, and analytical thinking; concerned with health, food, and community service; sensitive to criticism. In the body: pancreas, small intestine, spleen, and liver.

LIBRA (Air: cardinal) energetics: loves art and beauty for beauty's sake; focused on relationships, romance, harmony, cooperation—in other words, "we" oriented. In the body: lower back, kidneys, and bladder.

SCORPIO (Water: fixed) energetics: seeks solitude; focused on healing, sexuality, integration and disintegration, transformation and transmutation; prone to rethinking, manipulation, jealousy; increased psychic powers; intense and sometimes moody. In the body: reproductive organs, the colon.

SAGITTARIUS (Fire: mutable) energetics: upbeat, optimistic, lively, high energy, humorous, loves to travel and expand, confident, restless and needing freedom, prone to overspending and overdoing. In the body: thighs, sciatic nerve, and hips.

CAPRICORN (Earth: cardinal) energetics: sober, serious, cautious, grounded, history-oriented, structured, traditional, self-determined, prone to pessimism and negativity. In the body: knees, bones, teeth, skin.

AQUARIUS (Air: fixed) energetics: friendly, outgoing, visionary, revolutionary, radical, expressive of personal uniqueness. In the body: ankles, circulatory system, electrical forces in the body, and nerves in the spinal column.

PISCES (Water: mutable) energetics: spacey, dreamy, sometimes overindulgent, emotional, sentimental, empathetic, inward-facing, vulnerable, indecisive, needs time for pursuits of the imagination, strong psychic abilities. In the body: lymph, immunity, and the feet.

You'll notice that each of the signs has some words next to it in parentheses. The first word is the element currently associated with it. Refer back to your Elemental Alchemization course to remind yourself of the energies of each element. We'll talk more about these elemental designations, in general, tomorrow evening.

The second bit of parenthetical information is one of these three words:

* **cardinal**

* **fixed**

* **mutable**

To understand these nuggets, you need to recall that the tropical system used in Western astrology aligns with the seasons of the year. There are 12 quadrants of the zodiac and there are four seasons of the year, so each season is assigned three zodiac signs. Cardinal signs are where a new season begins. Those are Aries, Cancer, Libra, and Capricorn.

* The spring equinox begins the sun's transit through Aries (Fire).

* Summer solstice begins the sun's transit through Cancer (Water).

* The Autumn equinox begins the sun's transit through Libra (Air).

* Winter solstice begins the sun's transit through Capricorn (Earth).

(The element associated with each of these seasonal beginnings has never quite made sense to me, Firefly:

SPRING $\rightarrow$ Fire   SUMMER $\rightarrow$ Water   FALL $\rightarrow$ Air   WINTER $\rightarrow$ Earth

It neither aligns with my personal experience of the seasons nor with Aristotle's description of the elements. Water, which is assigned to Cancer, the initiatory sign for the summer season in astrology, is cold and wet in Aristotle's description of the elements. Keep this objection in mind for tomorrow evening's lesson!)

After the cardinal signs at the beginning of a new season, the sun tracks through a fixed, or stable, sign in the season's middle.

SPRING $\rightarrow$ Taurus   SUMMER $\rightarrow$ Leo   FALL $\rightarrow$ Scorpio   WINTER $\rightarrow$ Aquarius

Finally, before the season ends, the sun goes through the final quadrant, where things are already getting a little squiffy, or mutable, in advance of the seasonal change:

SPRING $\rightarrow$ Gemini   SUMMER $\rightarrow$ Virgo   FALL $\rightarrow$ Sagittarius   WINTER $\rightarrow$ Pisces

These seasonal movements are called *qualities*. They are the spice in your astrology chart, adding a nuanced flavor to each sign. You can look at your own chart to see if you have an abundance of a particular zodiac taste profile. If you do, it might tell you something about your personality (or it might not!).

* Cardinal signs are initiators. They are the signs that tend to get things moving and stir things up: Aries, Cancer, Libra, and Capricorn.

* Fixed signs are stabilizers. These signs resist change, which adds the effervescence of stability: Taurus, Leo, Scorpio, and Aquarius.

* Mutable signs are changeable, which can look a few different ways: they might be the change agents in their social circles, getting things moving and shaking, or they might be overly influenced by their environment and the energies around them, making them changeable themselves: Gemini, Virgo, Sagittarius, Pisces.

Each of these pieces of the puzzle—the zodiac sign, the element, and the quality, are the layers of the cake of your astrological chart.

Homework: Look at It Impersonally

In your next lesson, Firefly, you'll get a chance to see how all this applies to you. Before you do that, choose a sign that you don't think is in your chart. For instance, if you're an Aries choose Scorpio, or if you're a Capricorn pick Cancer. (If you are a more advanced student and know the entirety of your chart, choose a sign that you haven't already researched.)

Forgetting that I already gave you a description of the signs, write a description for your sign of choice based solely on its season, element, and quality. For instance, if you chose Aries, you would write a description based only on knowing that it's a springtime sign, that it is cardinal, and that it is a representative of the Fire element.

(Why do a sign that isn't in your chart? Because this time it's not about you, Firefly!)

Extra Credit

The word *zodiac* comes from the Greek *zodiakos kyklos* and *planet* comes from the Greek word *planetes*. Look up both . . . just another layer of symbolism, Firefly, to add to the magic of the Night.

Lesson 8:

MAKE IT PERSONAL
(A LESSON AND LAB ROLLED INTO ONE!)

In the moment of your birth, whether it was day or Night, the planets, sun, and moon (these last two are sometimes referred to in the classical texts by the lovely phrase "the luminaries"), were in a particular place in the sky. Certain constellations were visible, even if you couldn't see them with the naked eye. At that moment, the three signs that would dominate your chart were determined—your Sun, your Moon, and your Rising sign.

You probably already know your Sun sign. When someone asks you *What's your sign?* it's your Sun sign they're referring to. This is whatever quadrant was hanging like wallpaper behind the sun at the moment of your birth.

To learn your Moon and Rising signs, you can use an internet search. You'll need the date, time, and place of your birth—because astrology is still about time and place, Firefly.

Pop astrology has simplified the complexity of astrology down to your Sun sign. Pop astrology says, *Know your Sun sign, know you.* But, contrary to the dictates of pop astrology, the sun is not the all-supreme force in your chart. The sun has a dance partner named Luna. And, here's where it gets interesting, the sun teaches you about your yang, but the moon teaches you about your yin.

When you focus on your Sun sign, you're shining a light on the parts of you that are driven and outward, the bits of your personality that crave interaction with, and acknowledgment from, the social structures of the world. But what about the part of you that wants to stay home in your pajamas, drink tea, and reread *Pride and Prejudice* for the umpteenth time? When does she get a little love? And how do you learn more about her? By exploring your Moon sign. Your Moon sign is your Sun sign's dance partner, the yin to its yang, the jelly filling to its doughnut.

Your Rising sign is the constellation that was on the horizon when you were born. I like to think of it as the clothes you wear when you're out and about in the world. Those clothes say something about how you feel about yourself and how you want to be seen by others. They're also your armor and protection, both physically and metaphorically. Some astrologers say that reading the horoscope of your Rising sign is as important as reading the horoscope for your Sun sign. If you think about your Sun and Moon signs as defining your fundamental nature, while your Rising sign shows *how* that fundamental nature appears in the world, this advice makes good sense.

These three signs are a fabulous beginning point to peeling back the layers of your star chart. First look up your Sun, Moon, and Rising signs, then look at the descriptions of their energies, elemental associations, qualities, and associated body bits. This last one is interesting, Firefly. Remember that it's a focus on a particular part of your anatomy. A deeper dive into your chart by a skilled astrologer might reveal more, but for now go broad in your interpretation.

Think about what this information illuminates for you, and if balancing your sun and moon in your mind helps you see new aspects of yourself.

(This was a lesson and lab sandwich, Firefly, so there's no additional homework.)

Lesson 9:

THE CELESTIAL STEWPOT

I've read countless papers on ancient Babylonian and Hellenistic astrology to prepare for this lecture, Firefly. And what I found was not what I expected!

If you're familiar with basic astrology, you'll know that the 12 signs of the zodiac are grouped into what's called "triplicities" and that each triplicity is governed by an element. Like this:

FIRE:	EARTH:	AIR:	WATER:
Aries, Leo, Sagittarius	Taurus, Virgo, Capricorn	Gemini, Libra, Aquarius	Cancer, Scorpio, Pisces

You might be wondering, like I did, where these associations come from. And, specifically, what the role of Aristotle and Co. was in building them—if any . . . although I suspected there might be, because, as you'll remember, Aristotle was the social influencer of his day.

What I found as I traveled down the paper-strewn rabbit hole was celestial stew.

The cooking began when Alexander the Great conquered Persia in about 334 BCE and, in so doing, created the environment in which scholars from Greece, Egypt, and the Babylonian schools came together with bushels of ideas and loaves of tradition.

As with many other intellectual disciplines, thoughts about stargazing and astrology got thrown into a multicultural stewpot and the thinking of multiple philosophies were simmered together. The Babylonians brought the idea of exaltations (that means that celestial bodies have a quadrant of the sky in which they're happiest), the Greeks tossed in their gods, and the Egyptians contributed the concept of personal horoscopes.

This last one is interesting, because up until the Egyptians began looking at an individual's stars, astrology was reserved for the fates of cities, countries, and kings. These personal horoscopes became all the rage—proving that people have changed very little in the intervening millennia. But what was *not* the rage was using the four elements in astrology. In fact, in these early incarnations, the elemental associations don't appear at all. The zodiac was divided into triplicities, but they were governed not by the elements, but by the four winds associated with the cardinal compass points. (North, south, east, and west, just like on your compass, Firefly.)

In the case of astrology, our friend Aristotle seemed to have been an inhibitory presence. Remember that Aristotle's theory associated pairs of oppositions with the elements? Hot—>Cold, Wet—>Dry. While some astrologers were scribbling combos of the elements and the zodiac signs on their napkins, their scribbles were not aligning with Aristotle's theory, which was (at that time) unthinkable. And so, while the elements occasionally appear with the zodiac signs as early as the second century CE, the elemental pairings for each sign are thought to be a later addition to astrological lore.

So what was in the tasty celestial stew of the second century BCE? And why should we care?

Let me tackle why we should care first: astrology has always been both complex and mathematical. In the same way that alchemy is proto-chemistry, astrology is proto-astronomy. In addition to the fates of kings and city-states, ancient astrology was "predicting" exactly the types of events modern astronomers will happily claim as part of their science: the solstices, the equinoxes, when the sun would rise and set, and even when comets would appear in the sky.

In today's world, many consider astrology a Night art because it's not aligned with modern scientific principles. But I would argue that it is quintessentially day. Even if modern scientists don't agree with its rationale, astrology is still an ordered and highly mathematical system with rules and complexities, which leave little room for the pigtails and fuzzy slippers of the Night.

When we were studying alchemy, I said that *secret* is not the same as mystical. I would add here that *complex* is also not the same as mystical.

This is not to say that astrology can't be a Night art: only that, out of the box, the rules and regulations that govern its practice are about as high noon as they come. But everything has an opposite, Firefly, and the balance to the mathematically ordered aspects of astrology is often found in the people who practice it. The very best astrologers are both ridiculously intelligent and amusingly claircognizant. For them, traipsing through star charts, declinations, and stelliums energizes their precognition. The geometries created by the patterns of the stars whisper to them. The rigor and the layers of accrued meaning open the front door to daylight rationality but then allow them to slip straight out the back and into the Night.

But not all our brains are wired this way. So how can each of us claim a piece of the celestial spheres for ourselves? Sure, you can have one of these cosmic-claircognizants read your chart for you. But while that's fun and enlightening in the moment, it doesn't give you a personal practice of tracking the macro patterns of the heavens and interpreting how they influence your life and the world around you. Working with an astrologer doesn't give you the same sense of connection you get from stepping out under the stars and communing with the Night sky.

Which brings me back to: *what was in the tasty celestial stew of the second century BCE? Or how can we make things simple again?*

Because astrology has acquired its complexity over time, some of the intricacy is simply the sheer weight of thousands of years of thoughts. But some of it came about because technologies let us see and know more than ever before. The invention of the telescope let us see more planets. Computer programs let us run all kinds of charts with the click of a button.

We're overwhelmed by information, which, unless you're claircognizant, does not help you connect with the Night.

With that in mind, we'll be spending the remainder of this course exploring the aspects of astrology that can help you reconnect more directly with the Night.

How do you get back to looking up at the Night sky and using it as a metaphoric signpost that announces where you are, whether it's time for tea or a walk under the stars, and how far it is to the nearest boulangerie?

Homework: Think on It

Brainstorm at least 10 ways you can create a direct relationship for yourself with the Night sky.

Lesson 10:

SCRYING THE STARS

Let's shake off all that theory, Firefly!

I want you to do something super-simple: grab your compass, your star map, and a flashlight, then walk outside. (If you're day-reading, do this tonight.)

Use your compass to orient yourself.

Before you look up, set a question in your heart, the same way you did in your divination practice. Keep it simple like: *What message do you have for me tonight?* Or *what do I need to know about the coming weeks?*

Then . . . Look up.

What catches your eye first?

Hint: if it's moving, it's a planet, meteor, satellite, airplane, or space invaders. If this moving object was a primary focus for you, look to see which stars formed the wallpaper behind it. Then continue with the instructions below.

Based on the direction you're facing, you can use your star map to figure out which constellation waved to you. If you were drawn to a single star, see which constellation it's a part of.

Using a star map may be frustrating at first, just like reading a road map is more difficult if you don't have some idea of where you are. Mapping is a skill, and you'll get better with practice.

After you figure out which constellation has snagged your attention, head indoors and research its stories. As your read, think about how what you're learning is applicable to the question you asked. Interpret the star stories in the same way you would read a tarot or oracle card. (If you're feeling like your skills are rusty, that's a perfect excuse to review your divination lessons.)

A couple things to layer into your reading:

* If it was a moving object that called your attention to a particular region of the heavens, add the idea of motion and movement into the stewpot of your interpretation.

* If it was a single star that lit your eye, look at where that star sits in the larger constellation. What layers does this add to your thoughts?

Now it's time to experiment—because that's the best way to settle a head full of theory.

Try this exercise in a variety of ways:

* You could look to the east and see what constellation is rising, asking the question *what is rising in my own life?*

* Or you could look to the west and see what is setting, asking the question *what is setting in my own life?*

* Or you could look at the shapes formed by the stars, put on your Night-goggles, allow your eyes to go soft, and write your own story.

Homework: Try It

Go play!

Lesson 11:

HARNESSING THE LUNAR TIDES

The next two lessons introduce you to longer cycles and practices. You won't be able to get there and back in one Night. Read these lessons now and schedule time to practice them later.

The first practice, here in lesson 11, involves the moon. La Luna circles the earth every 29.5 days. Using your ephemeris to see the date of the next new moon, schedule 30 days to work through this lesson.

The moon is the closest of all the heavenly bodies to Earth.

Yes, obviously.

But it needs to be explicitly said to explain La Luna's impact on our planet. If you've ever stood on the shore watching the tide recede, you've witnessed the gravitational pull of the moon at play. The moon tugs at the tides, as well as the water table.

Put on your Night-goggles, Firefly, and think about what this factoid tells us. First, water is metaphorically associated with emotions. So moods are in the moon's domain.

Next, look at Aristotle's recipe for making a person:

Take a mix of air, earth, and fire.

Suspend it in a base of 60 percent water.

That's not a real Aristotelian recipe, but human adults *are* about 60 percent water. And it's not just us humans—all living things are comprised of a significant amount of water. So what if the moon is pulling *our* tides? What exactly might that look like?

Everyone and everything has the moon pulling at their internal waters, but there's no missing the effect in people who menstruate. The word *menstruation* comes from the Latin word *mensis*, which means "month," and is related to the Greek *mene*, which means "moon." But here's where it gets interesting: both *mensis* and *mene*, as well as words in Sanskrit, Slavonic, Lithuanian, Welsh, and Old Irish, are thought to come from the root *me*—which means "to measure." The measurement referred to was the length of the moon's phase, which often aligns with a menstrual cycle (especially when there's no artificial light involved—pure moonlight is better at creating hormonal cycles than electric lights).

So here we are, back to celestial objects as calendars. But it feels a bit more personal now, no? In prehistory, the moon was a timekeeper and those who menstruate were an earthly expression of her phases. So it's not surprising that, in the oldest tales, women represent time and destiny. The Moirai—the Greek Fates who wove each person's life thread and cut it when their destiny was done—were originally said to be the daughters of Nyx, which means "Night." There you have it, Firefly: time, fate, and destiny braided together into one cosmic challah.

To review:

* The moon's gravitation force pulls on large bodies of water.

* People are made, largely, of bodies of water.

* Therefore the moon pulls at people.

* Water represents emotion.

* People have emotions (sometimes large bodies of them).

* Therefore, metaphorically, the moon pulls at emotions, moving them in cycles like the tides.

* We can chart the effect of the lunar cycles on the tide.

*   Therefore we can chart the effects of the lunar cycle on our emotions. (Easier than connecting a lantern with a peacock!)

Homework: Chart Your Tides

Begin this exercise on a new moon. (Your ephemeris or Siri can tell you when the next new moon will be.) The moon will seem to grow larger and larger in the sky for the first 14 days (although we know she's staying the same size, just getting more reflected light from our friend the sun). The full moon marks the halfway point in the cycle. Then La Luna shrinks and shrinks until she's back to new. It's like a cosmic breath, Firefly, inhale, inhale, inhale until you're full then exhale, exhale, exhale back to emptiness.

Charting your moon tides will take 30 days. Each day, note the phase of the moon (you can just draw a little picture) along with how you're feeling. I recommend writing a short paragraph each day and then summarizing it in one word. Like this:

Today was awesome: I got so much done at work then got home and plowed through everything on my desk. My word: TRIUMPHANT!

Note: While you only need to do this for one month for your homework, you'll need to track multiple moon-ths to learn your own patterns and, by knowing them, be able to predict your moods. Just think about it, Firefly: what if you knew that you always felt *TRIUMPHANT* during the first quarter moon. Imagine the closet cleanups you could put right onto your calendar!

Extra Credit

Want to add another layer to the cosmic cake? Here's how:

Like the sun, the moon crosses through each of the quadrants of the zodiac. The sun takes about a month in each sign; La Luna moves faster, staying for only two and a half days or so in each quadrant.

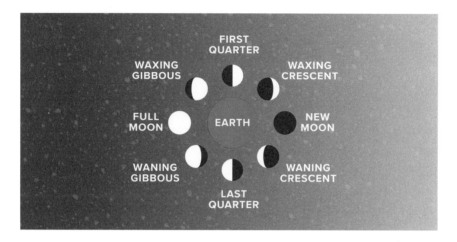

The moon mirrors the energy of the quadrant it's passing through. So, for instance, a new moon in Cancer is going to be super yin while a new moon in Aries will be a fabulous time to think about a new project. Use your ephemeris to layer the information about which sign the moon is in on top of the waxing and waning cycle and your record of your moods. This is also a fabulous opportunity to practice your calligraphy as you scribe the zodiac glyphs next to the little drawing of the moon. Here they are for reference:

♈ ARIES	♌ LEO	♐ SAGITTARIUS
♉ TAURUS	♍ VIRGO	♑ CAPRICORN
♊ GEMINI	♎ LIBRA	♒ AQUARIUS
♋ CANCER	♏ SCORPIO	♓ PISCES

As you layer the different resonances and meanings of each zodiac sign onto the moon's phase, you'll begin to see the depth and nuance of the information you're gathering. Maybe you are super-organized during the waxing moon . . . except when it's in Leo.

THE CYCLE OF RETURN

Ready to see the big picture, Firefly, and step into the macro patterns of the universe?

Before you say yes, consider the commitment. This is no mere hand-fasting that you can reconsider in a year and a day. Working with Jupiter takes 11½ years (at least) and engaging with Saturn takes 29.

If you haven't yet tackled a moon cycle, go back and do that first. La Luna makes fabulous training wheels for riding the larger cycles.

When you're cruising a cycle, whether moon or planetary, what you're looking for is patterns. With the shorter cycles like those of the moon, Mercury, or Venus, you can record your own trip, keeping good notes for yourself, so that when you ride the cycle again you can recognize emerging patterns. This lets you not only build on what you learned in the previous cycle, but divine what's coming next. For instance, if you pick a fight with your partner every full moon, you'll begin to realize that *full* is a volatile point in the moon's cycle for you. Once you understand that pattern, you can then predict that you'll fight with your partner on the next full moon and, if you want, do something to change your own future. That's divination at work, Firefly! It's also co-creation: once you know the recipe, you can improvise an ingredient or two. Maybe turn a fight into . . . *ahem*, I'm sure you have some ideas of how you can use that full moon energy.

Using your personal experience to guide you through a cycle is more difficult when you ride the long cycles of Jupiter or Saturn. You'll either need to practice extreme patience or do some research in the astrology annuals so you can understand what a typical cycle looks like.

Here are the planets you might consider working with when you're ready to make a long-term commitment. All of these planets are named for Roman gods and goddesses whose characteristics were said to infuse their namesakes.

* Mercury takes 88 days to circle the sun. Mercury was the messenger of the gods. Characterized as quick-witted, Mercury rules the mind and intellect, travel, luck, and divination.

* Venus's circuit takes 9 months, which seems an appropriate amount of time for the goddess of love to gestate. Venus was the patron of both lovers and prostitutes, as much about fertility and the act of love as the emotion of love. In astrology, Venus is associated with joy and happiness as well as *amore*.

* Mars takes 2½ years to circumnavigate the sun. Mars was the god of war, but he was also the god of farming. War was a destabilizing force, which was, ultimately, meant to lead to greater stability by conquering more land to farm, which meant a more secure source of food. So, while volatile, Mars is not purposelessly violent.

* Jupiter, the sky father, takes 11½ years to circle the sun. An air god, Jupiter was the equivalent of the Greek god Zeus. He was involved in governance and justice, philosophy and righteousness. His were the systems that kept empires ticking smoothly along.

* Saturn takes 29 years, making a Saturn return a much-anticipated event. Some say Saturn was based on the Etruscan god Satre, a god of wealth and plenty, associated with renewal, liberation, peace,

and plenty. But the Saturn that we see in astrology is based on the Greek god Chronos, the rather vicious god of time. In astrology, the bands of the planet Saturn also make a metaphoric appearance, giving Saturn's energy an air of constriction.

Back when Ptolemy was writing the books that would become the primers on astrology for millennia to come (those books are noted in the resources section, Firefly), these were the known planets. The others were out there, of course, but only the sharpest eyes could see them because the telescope was not yet invented. These classical planets work for our purposes, since the planets further out have cycles that are a bit excessive—unless you've been practicing your alchemy and have discovered the philosopher's stone, which, of course, changes everything.

Because Jupiter and Saturn return so rarely, they were seen as a pair in classical times and given the superhero name the Great Chronocrator, from the Greek *chronos*, meaning "time." This pair was said to make an appearance to mark significant events—like the birth of a particular baby that swapped the calendar from BC to AD. The Star of Bethlehem is thought to be the Great Chronocrator making an appearance.

Homework: Contemplate the Long Game

If you're ready, begin tracking one of the long-cycle planets through your own life. Pair the aspects of the planet with your tracking to, for instance, record an intellectual history while tracking Mercury or your own love story while tracking Venus. In the same way that you make a few daily notes in your moon journal, to track one of the planets, simply take a few daily notes! (Life is complex enough without making this complicated, Firefly.) The cycle can begin today and will end in the time designated in the list above. The first cycle lays the foundation. It's by recording subsequent cycles that you'll begin to see your patterns.

If this type of commitment is too much right now, take this opportunity to explore stories about the planets from around the globe. What other names do these planets have? How might other tales about them affect how you use them in your personal astrology?

ADDITIONAL READINGS AND RESOURCES

For the "I-know-nothing beginner," these books make a great starting point:

The Only Astrology Book You'll Ever Need by Joanna Martine Woolfolk

The Stars Within You: A Modern Guide to Astrology by Juliana McCarthy

The Inner Sky by Steven Forrest

The Only Way to Learn Astrology by Marion D. March and Joan McEvers

The Essential Guide to Practical Astrology by April Elliott Kent

You Were Born for This by Chani Nicholas

Interested in sidereal (Vedic) astrology? These are for you:

An Introduction to Western Sidereal Astrology by Kenneth Bowser

Gate & Key by G. Desiree Fultz

For a cross-cultural look at the constellations, check out *Figures in the Sky*, an interactive website that shows you the constellation systems of 28 "sky cultures." https://figuresinthesky.visualcinnamon.com

Looking for star stories? You'll find them in these beautiful books:

Written in the Stars by Alison Davies

Seeing Stars by Sara Gillingham

The children's section of the bookstore or library is another fabulous resource for multicultural star stories.

If you want to travel the world finding ancient astronomical observatories and temples aligned with the path of the sun, be sure to take along *Atlas Obscura* by Joshua Foer, Dylan Thuras, and Ella Morton.

An article called "Astronomy and Cosmology at Angkor Wat," by Robert Stencel, Fred Gifford, and Eleanor Morón was published in *Science* magazine in 1976. What's fascinating about this article is that it was published during the terror reign of the Khmer Rouge. At that time, Cambodia was not open to foreign visitors. This article was written based on extensive study of the plans, as well as older photographs. What was discovered was that, in addition to being an observatory, Angkor Wat has historical, calendrical, and mythological data encoded into its measurements.

I've never met astrologer Chris Brennan, but his various articles on Hellenistic astrology are both readable and complete. He has a book called *Hellenistic Astrology: The Study of Fate and Fortune,* which is on my "to read" list.

If you're going to deep dive into astrology and want to understand the history, Ptolemy is the wellspring. His books *Almagest* and *Tetrabiblos* have both been translated into English. I can't give you a rating on the density meter, Firefly, as these books are far too mathematical for my non-geometric brain.

When you're working with the long cycle of Saturn, this book might be helpful: *Saturn: A New Look at an Old Devil,* by Liz Greene.

office hours

COME ON IN, FIREFLY.

That was quite a journey! It's okay to put your feet up; I'm tired too. But it's the good kind of tired, like after you've spent an entire weekend organizing the attic.

You heard me question some aspects of modern astrology, and maybe, through your studies, you realized that some of the foundational bits of ancient star lore don't align as perfectly with your modern beliefs as you thought they would. I don't blame you if, at this point, you just want a simple answer: *is astrology true and good and real, or is it just another one of the beautiful fallacies we've seen on our tour through mystical history?*

That's the cosmic question, isn't it? I'm not going to offer an answer (as answers are yours to find) but I do have a few things for you to consider as you contemplate your ongoing relationship with the celestial spheres: first, the difficulties we humans have in understanding long cycles and patterns; second, the power of thoughts and images embedded in the cultural psyche; and finally, the definition of a right answer.

Let's start with thinking about macro patterns—the patterns that happen over a span of time, or in a span of space, that we can't quite grasp. To the average day-brain it would seem that knowing the placement of the stars at the moment of your birth is frippery and nothing more. But a daytimer who had studied complex systems might give the concept of astrology a smidge more credence. In a complex system, cause and effect are distant from each other in both time and space.

Complex systems can be hard to understand, so let's get warmed up by looking at simple systems. Children (and wolf cubs and baby hawks) learn through simple systems of cause and effect: touch a hot stove—> burn your hand. The cause (the hot stove) and the effect (your burnt hand) are near to each other in both time and space. Remember, this is a simple system, not a complex one: your hand and the stove are physically proximate; the cause (touching the stove) initiates the effect (the burn) in mere moments. As I said, this is a simple system. There are zillions of simple systems in your everyday life, and they tend to feel pretty far away from the realms of magic and mystery: you pay your parking fee, the gate goes up and lets you out of the lot; you drive to the end of the street, the traffic light turns red, you stop; someone needs to make a left out of the grocery store lot, you pause to let them through, you get a wave. (This one doesn't always work as expected!)

But now imagine how much difficulty you would have understanding cause and effect if you were walking to the coffee shop and, back home, someone turned on the stove and your hand started to burn. There you are standing on the corner of Spruce and 4th with your hand burning up. *What?!* That makes no sense. You were nowhere near the stove, how could it possibly be burning your hand? That sounds suspiciously like magic!

But I'm not saying that your stove at home can burn your hand when you aren't near it, Firefly. What I am saying is that in complex systems the cause and effect are distant from each other in the same way. The classic example of this is the butterfly beating its wings in Schenectady and somehow causing a storm, seven weeks later, in Singapore. The wingbeats and storm are distant from each other in both time and space. Because of this distance, we don't see a clear correlation. There isn't a feedback loop that helps us understand, respond, or change our (or the butterfly's) behavior.

The planets, which are mapped in your astrological chart, are distant in both time and space. It's almost impossible, over the course of one lifetime, to correlate the effects they might have on our lives. Knowing in our heads that we live in an interconnected universe is not the same as seeing it in our daily lives, feeling it with our hearts, and experiencing interconnection with our bodies. If every time Mars entered your chart your hand burned, it would be easier to believe that Mars affected your life.

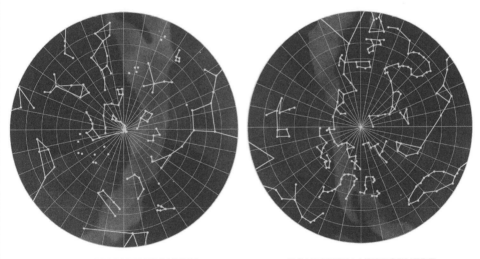

NORTHERN HEMISPHERE   SOUTHERN HEMISPHERE

So how can you know if it works? If you need to know in an instant, I'm afraid your only option is faith and belief, Firefly. But if you're willing to treat it like an experiment, you can work with the cycles in the last two lessons. Over time, you'll develop your very own opinion—and as you know, I think well-developed personal opinions are the best kinds of opinions.

Speaking of opinions, you'll probably have one on this next point, but before you jump in to opine, put on your Night-goggles and sit with what I'm saying. And remember that, even by the light of day, the experimenter affects the experiment. Here goes: thoughts and images embedded in our cultural psyche, the ones that are strong enough to take up residence in the C.U., are powerful enough to affect the experiment that is human history . . . and maybe even strong enough to create resonance with the stars.

In essence, is it possible that a millennia of accumulated belief has altered the fundamental nature of the universe? Dream on that, Firefly!

Finally, your original question reminds me of a conversation I had with my geometry tutor many years ago. He had just handed me a test with an oversized red *D* written across the top.

He began going over the test, showing us the correct answers. *Wait!* I said, after he put the answer to the first proof on the board. *That's the answer I got!* I held up my test to show him.

Yes, you got the right answer, he said. *But you got to it the wrong way.*

In the daylight world, if you get the right answer but you get to it the wrong way, you get a *D.*

But in the Night? Well, that's a whole different story.

final exams

It's time to assimilate what you've learned, so you can see your own life through the lens of the mystic. We often think that magic lives outside of ourselves; that it's happening all the time for other people (perhaps you can think of someone you follow on social media you're *sure*, based on their darkly evocative photographs, is living a life more magical than your own).But you have learned how to step wholly into the Night— its magic is waiting for you to connect with it!

The next stage of your studies is to recognize the synchronicities and guidance of the Night in your daytime life. Once you do this, you'll realize Night-thoughts and daydreams are like pepper jack and cheddar: two cheeses in the same delicious casserole. Take a bite so you can enjoy all the creamy goodness life has to offer!

This final exam will encourage you to reframe the dualities of your life and find its patterns, both large and small. It will help you recognize that what may seem like a bunch of separate ingredients has actually alchemized into a hearty meal.

How are we going to work this magic?

You're going to craft an essay using a structure explained by a wise man named Joseph Campbell. Campbell looked at hundreds of myths and origin stories from around the globe and analyzed their components, finding the common threads. From this universal structure, he laid out what is called the *Hero's Journey* or the *monomyth*. It's a map for finding the mythic patterns not only in the stories around you but in your own life. I like to think of it as a magic mirror that allows you to catch a glimpse of your own archetypical self.

Some people have said that the Hero's Journey best applies to those who identify as male. But that's a rather literal read. When you put on your Night-goggles, remember your dualities, and allow each step on the journey to be a star-sprinkled metaphor; it works fine for just about anyone. (Still, I'll put some books in the library written by people who disagree with me, so you have the tools to come to your very own conclusion. Developing one's very own conclusion is always far more interesting than merely accepting mine.)

To complete your Night School studies, your final mission, should you choose to accept it, is to craft a piece of your own mythology. You'll take one event or period of your life, pull out your compass, put on your Night-goggles, and retell it as a Hero's Journey. Grand, isn't it?

Let's first talk about why this project is a fantabulous final exam:

* **First, you will find the patterns at work in your own life. Refer to Midnight Foundations to remind you of some of the universal patterns at play.**

* **In order to work with the Hero's Journey, you'll need to reframe hardships into learning experiences, testing the skills you learned in the Mysteries of Being Human.**

* **The Hero's Journey is all about the alchemy of personal transformation, mirroring what you discovered in Elemental Alchemization.**

* **This exercise will help you notice when you're flowing with the tides**

of your life and when you're out of sync. You can use this as a launching pad for the extra-credit assignment of comparing your life's story with the cycles of the moon and your astrology chart to understand when in your life you've been Harnessing the Celestial Tides . . . and when you haven't. (It feels so good to go with your own flow, Firefly.)

* And, finally, you can use the Tools of the Mystic to divine what's next. (Or use your pendulum to find something you lost along the way. I once found a stone that had fallen out of my aunt's ring using a pendulum and a bit of sympathetic magic. More important than stuff lost along the way, you may realize that you lost yourself, or an important piece of you. The pendulum isn't the best tool for this retrieval, instead try dream work or active imagining. Go back to the place where you got lost; from there, you're sure to be found.)

Now that you understand the whys of what we're doing, let's talk about the *whats* and the *hows*.

Joseph Campbell's Hero's Journey looks like this:

The hero (that's you, Firefly) begins in the ordinary world or what I like to call Mundania. Life might be lovely or bleh, comfortable or laden with difficulties. Then one day, the hero is called to an adventure. In our modern world, this might be a job offer or an invitation to take a trip (in myths, it usually involved being asked to save a city or slay a dragon) but the hero (again, that's you) says, "No thanks. I'm good. Find somebody else."

At this point, the hero might remain forever embedded in their current situation, if it were not for the appearance of a mentor or teacher who helps them see why this adventure might be fun, worthwhile, or just the thing to get them out of some dark and dreadful funk. While this mentor might be a Yoda-type character, most often in our modern tales it's a best friend or parent or even a stranger on the subway who says something

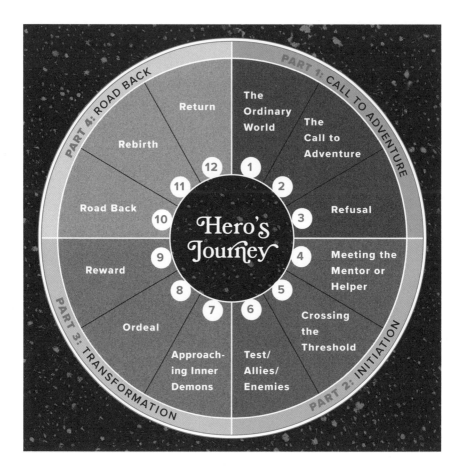

that smells like jasmine and tastes like synchronicity. This allows you, our hero, to cross the threshold into the adventure to come.

But it's not so easy—there's resistance. Maybe in your moment of hesitation the job was offered to someone else or the flight to the fabulous vacation destination sold out (or, if you're in a classic myth, there's some monster guarding the gate that needs a good slaying). Moving through this first ordeal is an initiation process (something you'll find, if you continue studying the ways of the Night, will come up often).

The next step of the journey is where you, our hero, begin to change, evolve, and grow because of what you're experiencing. This is the section of the story in which the life-changing conflict or decision takes place. And, once you are transformed by this event, you reap the rewards of your efforts. In myth, this is the final battle with the dragon and the subsequent discovery of the Ruby of Indwolem (which I just totally made up so don't try an internet search). In more modern tales, this is often an inward-facing moment: the discovery of a fortitude, resolve, or intelligence you didn't know you had. It's the moment when you realize you are more capable than you had previously thought or that you actually possess the traits you've long admired in others—that the gold that makes them sparkle also glints within you. So at the new job, you take on a project you didn't think you could handle, or on the trip, you realize that you've been hiding a secret from both yourself and your partner.

The final sequence of the Hero's Journey is the return home. In this final act, you have to figure out how to return to your old life as your new self. So if, on your trip, you realized that you'd prefer to be with someone of a different gender, this last section of the journey would involve going home and having the tough conversation with your current partner. (Yes, it would be lovely to stay in Greece with the hottie who helped you come to this epiphany, but you'd be missing the final growth moment, which lets you integrate this episode into the larger scope of your life.)

And that, Firefly, is the cycle of the Hero's Journey. (Note that like the alchemical cycle, you are back at the first element, Earth—your home ground—and ready to do the whole dance all over again.)

Now let's talk about the *how* of turning your Hero's Journey into your final exam. This will be a three-step process.

STEP 1:

IDENTIFY THE HERO'S JOURNEY IN THE WILD

Watch a movie of your choice and map the Hero's Journey through the story line. To see and begin to recognize the pattern, it's easiest to start with epic adventures like *Star Wars*, *The Princess Bride*, *The Hunger Games*, or *Spider-Man* but just about any movie that played on a main stage will do.

Some art house editions purposely break out of the Hero's Journey mode. (Anything—even a good story structure—can become a straight-jacket, Firefly.) If you feel vaguely unsatisfied when you reach *The End*, like there was no conclusion to the story, or if you spend the whole movie saying, *I don't get it. Nothing's happening,* then you are most likely watching something avant-garde that's experimenting with being an anti-story. These movies won't work for this exercise.

STEP 2:

GET YOUR HERO'S JOURNEY OUT OF
YOUR HEAD AND INTO THE WORLD

It's time to turn a piece of your own life's story into a Hero's Journey.

How you approach this next step will be personal and will depend upon how you prefer to express yourself. If you're someone who loves to write, this might be a long-form story. But that is far from the only option! It could be a series of collages, paintings, or videos. Perhaps it's a story-board, where each leg of the journey is noted in a few words and has an image that goes along with it. Maybe you draw your Hero's Journey out as a graphic novel, or write it as a play or screenplay.

What I would advise is to avoid choosing a form that is so intimidating you don't get it done. If you want to write a screenplay, then storyboard it and turn in your storyboard to receive credit for your final exam. You can complete the larger project later—and it will be all the better for having been mapped out first.

STEP 3:

IDENTIFY THE PATTERNS

The final piece of the final exam process is to go back into your story, after you have expressed it, and look for these things:

* signs of the alchemical cycle at play

* inklings of the macro patterns weaving through your own story

* any foundational principles which you might be exploring through the actions in your own life

* and decisive moments of foresight and synchronicity which craft your path forward

In order to complete your studies at the Night School, your Final Exam is due to your journal two weeks after you receive this assignment.

(As with most things in life, Firefly, it's more important to do it than to do it perfectly. We're on a pass/fail system here and the only way to fail is not to do it.)

Extra Credit

After you have identified the patterns within your own story, go back and see if they align with movements in your personal astrology chart or, if your story takes place over a shorter period of time, with the phases of the moon.

Commendation
from the Night Mistress

Please deliver this to the front desk at the C.U. Library.

Most esteemed Madam:

Please allow this letter to serve as a certification of completion of all coursework and exams offered at the Night School.

All circles have been squared, permutations have been perambulated, and as many synchronicities as possible have been simultaneously situated. The bearer knows how to get there and back in just one Night and can use all four elements to make a stellar Bananas Foster. (Plus they understand that it's best to do this when they have the fifth element waiting in their stomach.)

Additionally, the bearer is certified to be skilled in the use of their compass, Night-goggles, and pendulum, and they have a full basket of bread crumbs (crumbled from a most excellent sourdough baguette) to mark their way in case of emergency.

In my estimation, they are fully prepared to enter the inner sanctums and should be issued a pass immediately.

Yours in Starlight,

Beatrice Marlow,

The Night Mistress

You did it, Firefly! Welcome to the ranks of the Night School alumni. The Night awaits!

Yours—

Bea

Notes from the Teachers' Lounge

This book began with the words *the Night School*. They lodged in my brain and refused to budge. I phoned my assistant (which is an unfortunately diminutive word for the person who knows more about my business than I do and has held my hand through all of the ups and downs of being an author) and said excitedly "*The Night School!*"

"Okay. What is it?" she replied doubtfully.

At the time I didn't know: Was it an email series? An online community? A book?

But whatever it was going to be, it was clear that the Night School had just had its Big Bang moment: it had been sparked into existence. And Shannon Thayer was there to catch the creation as it poured from deep within me and splashed down disruptively in the middle of our workday. Thanks for attending the birth, Shan (you're getting rather good at midwifing!).

The journey from "*Aha!*" to published book takes many minds, hearts, and hands. But it always starts with my agent, Laura Lee Mattingly, giving the project the thumbs-up. If I can convince Laura Lee, I'm 90 percent there. I used to read the thank-yous in the backs of books and feel jealous of other authors' relationships with their agents. I don't have to go green anymore. Thank you, Laura Lee, for wading into my never-ending stream of ideas, for always having my back, and for guiding me through the rapids of the book publishing industry. Special thanks for hooking me up with Shannon Connors Fabricant at Running Press; Bea would not exist without her!

The idea for Bea came late in the game. I got an email from a Night Schooler (because I tried all the ideas—book, email series, and community) who reminded me about "The School of the Night": a group of rebel thinkers including Sir Walter Raleigh, Christopher Marlowe, George Chapman, Matthew Roydon, and Thomas Harriot, who met in the late 1500s to discuss philosophy and science. Of course, I had heard of the School of the Night (if you've read Deborah Harkness's Discovery of Witches series, so have you), but I'd forgotten about them. The mention sent me off on a research binge. The research binge led to the thought, *Hmm . . . what if the School of the Night continued on in secret? What if each headmaster took on the last name of one of the founders?* And thus Beatrice Marlowe was born. But, if it weren't for my spectacular editor Shannon Connors Fabricant, Bea would have remained quietly in the background. I will be forever grateful that Shannon was unfazed by the idea of a nonfiction book being narrated by a fictional character (which probably seems perfectly acceptable now that we've done it, but it was genre-bending as a concept).

And Bea deserves thanks too. She quickly became my inspiration and my muse. There were times when I engaged in a practice my husband dubbed "method writing"—a riff on "method acting"—becoming Bea so I could understand how she thought and felt. I ate banana and peanut butter sandwiches for breakfast (Bea seems inordinately fond of bananas), redecorated my office with mismatched Persian rugs and orchids (all white), and bought myself a microscope. I knew Bea had become real when my friends referred to her as if she were a well-loved member of our crew: "What would Bea say?" they'd muse or "Bea would know what to do!"

It was most gratifying when the team at Running Press fell for Bea, too. Big thanks to everyone at RP who put their faith in Bea and the Night School. A book is always a team effort and I appreciate each and every one of you. An infinite amount of gratitude to artist Lucille Clerc and book designer Susan Van Horn for making these pages visually luscious. Special thanks to Melanie Gold, Ada Zhang, and Ashley Benning for meticulous detail and production work. Betsy Hulsebosch, Jessica Schmidt, Amy Cianfrone, and Kara Thornton: deep bows for your efforts to share *The Night School* with the wider world.

Getting the manuscript for this book written during the year that we were all coping with the COVID-19 pandemic was an all-hands-on-deck affair. My local writing group met straight through the winter, sitting socially distanced outdoors with blankets and extra-large cups of tea (it will be remembered as the winter I got everyone addicted to London Fogs). Huge thanks to Steph Jagger, Sarah Selecky, Carrie Frye, and Paige Gilchrist, who rallied to read the manuscript, over and over, as I honed both the content and Bea's voice. You are all priceless to me. Hugs and high fives: we did it!

What a writer needs most is time to write, so big thanks to Alison, Heidi, and Kate for making sure my other responsibilities were completely covered (like I-don't-even-have-to-think-about-it covered, which is a tremendous gift).

Andrew, as always, thanks for being my partner in all ways. Each time I sit down to write I'm grateful for this life we've created that lets both of us live our dreams.

Finally, thanks for reading, Firefly. Truly, there are no books without you!

The Night School Library

Welcome to the Night School Library, Firefly! My reading suggestions are compiled here for easy perusal (and I *may* have added a few extras beyond what's in the Additional Resources lists!).

Check out whatever books you want, for as long as you want. May they ignite your imagination in the ways that they have inspired my own.

ORIENTATION

Gather Your Supplies

Basho, Matsuo. *On Love and Barley: Haiku of Basho*. Translated by Lucien Stryk. Penguin Classics, 1986.

—— *Basho's Haiku: Selected Poems of Matsuo Basho*. Translated by David Landis Barnhill. SUNY Press, 2004.

Goldberg, Natalie. *Three Simple Lines: A Writer's Pilgrimage into the Heart and Homeland of Haiku*. New World Library, 2021.

SEMESTER 1

Midnight Foundations (Philosophy 101)

Aurelius, Marcus. *Meditations: A New Translation*. Translated by Gregory Hays. Modern Library, 2002.

Heraclitus. *Fragments: The Collected Wisdom of Heraclitus*. Translated by Brooks Haxton. Viking Adult, 2001.

Lightman, Alan. *Einstein's Dreams*. Vintage Books, 2004.

Lounsbury, Floyd G., and Bryan Gick. *The Oneida Creation Story*. University of Nebraska Press 2000.

Ni, Maoshing. *The Yellow Emperor's Classic of Medicine: A New Translation of the Neijing Suwen with Commentary*. Shambhala, 1995.

Rajpoot, Govind. *Interpretation of the CHARAKA SAMHITA Volume 1a/10: Sutrasthan (1A)*. University of Ayurveda, Prague, 2016.

Robbins, Tom. *Jitterbug Perfume*. Bantam Books, 1990.

Secundus, Gaius Plinius (Pliny the Elder). *Natural History: A Selection*. Penguin Classics, 1991.

Tzu, Lao. *Tao Te Ching*. Translated by Stephen Mitchell. Harper Perennial, 1994.

The Mysteries of Being Human (Psychology 101)

Beck, Martha. *Finding Your Own North Star: Claiming the Life You Were Meant to Live*. Harmony, 2002.

—— *Steering by Starlight: The Science and Magic of Finding Your Destiny*. Rodale Books, 2008.

Damasio, Antonio. *Descartes' Error: Emotion, Reason and the Human Brain*. Vintage Books, 2006.

Das, Lama Surya. *Make Me One with Everything: Buddhist Meditations to Awaken from the Illusion of Separation*. Sounds True, 2015.

Khalsa, Hari Kaur. *A Woman's Book of Meditation: Discovering the Power of a Peaceful Mind*. Avery, 2006.

Lipton, Bruce H. *The Biology of Belief: Unleashing the Power of Consciousness, Matter & Miracles*. Hay House, 2010.

Mardell, Ashley. *The ABCs of LGBT+*. Mango, 2016.

Menakem, Resmaa. *My Grandmother's Hands: Racialized Trauma and the Pathway to Mending Our Hearts and Bodies*. Central Recovery Press, 2017.

Mountain Dreamer, Oriah. *The Invitation*. HarperOne, 2006.

Pert, Candace B. *Molecules of Emotion: The Science Behind Mind-Body Medicine*. Simon & Schuster, 1999.

Rothman, Julia, and Shaina Feinberg. *Every Body: An Honest and Open Look at Sex from Every Angle*. Voracious, 2021.

Divining the Night (Divination 101)

Adams, Douglas. *The Ultimate Hitchhiker's Guide to the Galaxy*. Del Rey, 2002.

Alighieri, Dante. *The Divine Comedy of Dante Alighieri: The Inferno*. Translated by James Romanes Sibbald. Lector House, 2019.

Gilbert, Elizabeth. *The Signature of All Things: A Novel*. Riverhead Books, 2014.

Johnson, Robert A. *Inner Work: Using Dreams and Active Imagination for Personal Growth*. HarperCollins, 1986.

—— *Owning Your Own Shadow: Understanding the Dark Side of the Psyche*. HarperSanFrancisco, 1994.

Jung, Carl Gustav. *Selected Letters of C.G. Jung, 1909–1961*. Edited by Gerhard Adler & Aniela Jaffé. Princeton University Press, 2014.

Krans, Kim. *The Wild Unknown Archetypes Deck and Guidebook*. HarperOne, 2019.

Ohashi, Wataru, and Tom Monte. *Reading the Body: Ohashi's Book of Oriental Diagnosis*. Penguin Books, 1991.

Shlain, Leonard. *The Alphabet Versus the Goddess: The Conflict Between Word and Image*. Penguin Books, 1999.

SEMESTER 2

Elemental Alchemization (Alchemy 101)

Aristotle. *On the Heavens*. CreateSpace Independent Publishing Platform, 2014.

Bartlett, Robert Allen. *Real Alchemy: A Primer of Practical Alchemy*. Ibis, 2009.

Cunningham, Scott. *Earth, Air, Fire & Water: More Techniques of Natural Magic*. Llewellyn Publications, 2002.

Euclid. *Euclid's Elements*. Translated by T. L. Heath. Green Lion Press, 2002.

Gilbert, Elizabeth. *Big Magic: Creative Living Beyond Fear*. Penguin Publishing Group, 2016.

Jung, Carl Gustav. *Modern Man in Search of a Soul*. Translated by W. S. Dell. Martino Fine Books, 2017.

—— *Psychology and Alchemy (Collected Works of C.G. Jung Vol. 12)*. Translated by Gerhard Adler and R.F.C. Hull. Princeton University Press, 1980.

Junius, Manfred. *Spagyrics: The Alchemical Preparation of Medicinal Essences, Tinctures, and Elixirs*. Healing Arts Press, 2007.

Kraig, Donald Michael. *Modern Magick: Twelve Lessons in the High Magickal Arts*. Llewellyn Publications, 2010.

Levi-Strauss, Claude. *The Raw and the Cooked (Mythologiques)*. University of Chicago Press, 1983.

Morris, Richard. *The Last Sorcerers: The Path from Alchemy to the Periodic Table*. Joseph Henry Press, 2003.

Nosrat, Samin. *Salt, Fat, Acid, Heat: Mastering the Elements of Good Cooking*. Simon & Schuster, 2017.

Plato. *Timaeus*. Translated by Benjamin Jowett. Independently published, 2020.

Pollan, Michael. *Cooked: A Natural History of Transformation*. Penguin Books, 2014.

Starhawk. *The Spiral Dance: A Rebirth of the Ancient Religion of the Goddess: 20th Anniversary Edition*. HarperOne, 1999.

Harnessing the Celestial Tides (Energetic Engineering 101)

Bowser, Kenneth. *An Introduction to Western Sidereal Astrology*. American Federation of Astrologers, 2016.

Brennan, Chris. *Hellenistic Astrology: The Study of Fate and Fortune*. Amor Fati Publications, 2017.

Davies, Alison. *Written in the Stars: Constellations, Facts and Folklore*. Quadrille Publishing, 2018.

Foer, Joshua, Dylan Thuras, and Ella Morton. *Atlas Obscura: An Explorer's Guide to the World's Hidden Wonders*. Workman Publishing Company, 2016.

Forrest, Steven. *The Inner Sky: How to Make Wiser Choices for a More Fulfilling Life*. Seven Paws Press, 2012.

Fultz, G. Desiree. *Gate & Key: Sidereal 13 Sign Astrology*. CreateSpace Independent Publishing Platform, 2018.

Gillingham, Sara. *Seeing Stars: A Complete Guide to the 88 Constellations*. Phaidon Press, 2018.

Greene, Liz. *Saturn: A New Look at an Old Devil*. Weiser Books, 2011.

Kent, April Elliott. *The Essential Guide to Practical Astrology: Everything from Zodiac Signs to Prediction, Made Easy and Entertaining*. Two Moon Publishing, 2016.

March, Marion D., and Joan McEvers. *The Only Way to Learn Astrology, Volume 1*. ACS Publications, 2008.

McCarthy, Juliana. *The Stars Within You: A Modern Guide to Astrology*. Roost Books, 2018.

Nicholas, Chani. *You Were Born for This: Astrology for Radical Self-Acceptance*. HarperOne, 2021.

Ptolemy, Claudius. *The Almagest: Introduction to the Mathematics of the Heavens*. Translated by Bruce M. Perry. Green Lion Press, 2014.

—— *Tetrabiblos*. CreateSpace Independent Publishing Platform, 2015.

Woolfolk, Joanna Martine. *The Only Astrology Book You'll Ever Need*. Taylor Trade Publishing, 2012.

FINAL EXAMS

Blackie, Sharon. *If Women Rose Rooted: A Life-changing Journey to Authenticity and Belonging*. September Publishing (UK), 2019.

Campbell, Joseph. *The Hero with a Thousand Faces (The Collected Works of Joseph Campbell)*. New World Library, 2008.

Campbell, Joseph, and Bill Moyers. *The Power of Myth*. Anchor, 1991.

Murdock, Maureen. *The Heroine's Journey: Woman's Quest for Wholeness*. Shambhala, 2020.

Tatar, Maria. *The Heroine with 1001 Faces*. Liveright, 2021.

Volger, Christopher. *The Writer's Journey—25th Anniversary Edition: Mythic Structure for Writers*. Michael Wiese Productions, 2020.

ADDITIONAL RESOURCES

Toll, Maia. *The Illustrated Herbiary*. Storey, 2018.

—— *The Illustrated Bestiary*. Storey, 2019.

—— *The Illustrated Crystallary*. Storey, 2020.

—— *Maia Toll's Wild Wisdom Companion*. Storey, 2021.

Index

The Author

MAIA TOLL is the author of the *The Illustrated Herbiary, The Illustrated Bestiary, The Illustrated Crystallary,* and *The Wild Wisdom Companion.*

Maia lives in the mountains of Asheville, North Carolina, with her partner, two ridiculously spoiled dogs, and an uninterrupted stretch of the night sky. You can find her at maiatoll.com and visit her herb shops in Asheville, NC; Philadelphia, PA; or online at herbiary.com.

The Headmistress

BEATRICE MARLOWE blew in on a winter wind that whipped down the mountains and scattered the last of the autumn leaves. Fully formed, like Venus arriving on the half-shell or Athena springing from Zeus's head, Bea dubbed herself the Night Mistress, made a cup of tea, and installed herself in front of the computer. The rest, as they say, is history.

southern
hemisphere

CANIS
MAJO

PISCIS
VOLANS

CRATER

CRUX
(SOUTHERN CROSS)

CORVUS

CENTAURUS

CIRCINUS

ARA

VIRGO

LUPUS

SCORPIO

LIBRA